Mary Baker Eddy

A centennial appreciation

A series of articles reprinted
from *The Christian Science Journal,*
January to December — 1966

Mary Baker Eddy

A centennial appreciation

THE CHRISTIAN SCIENCE PUBLISHING SOCIETY
Boston, Massachusetts

Library of Congress Card Number 67-16977

Printed in the United States of America

Foreword

During the Centennial Year of the discovery of Christian Science a series of twelve articles was presented in *The Christian Science Journal* and the French and German editions of *The Herald of Christian Science* on certain aspects of the distinguished lifework of Mary Baker Eddy. This book is a reprint of those articles.

Each article was written by an outstanding Christian Scientist whose individual background and experience qualified him or her to bring out something of the many-faceted experiences of the Discoverer and Founder of Christian Science.

It would be impossible for any book to deal adequately and in total with the diversity of talents and abilities which characterizes Mrs. Eddy's extraordinary lifework. Her abilities as an author, as a preacher, as a practitioner in the healing ministry, as an organizer and leader of a great religious movement, all shine through the articles in this series, but they only hint at the significance of her lifework and her great contribution to all mankind.

Contents

1

Mary Baker Eddy
Her fulfillment of prophecy

by Julia M. Johnston

Century has followed century nineteen times since the man of Nazareth uttered holy words which he prophesied would never pass away. They have hung in the thoughts of men like music of the spheres. They have been heard with awe and reverence, but their vast Science has remained to be discovered in this age.

True prophecy bears the seed of fulfillment which matures in appointed time. Isaiah foretold the coming of Christ Jesus, which occurred about seven hundred years later. The prophecy of the Master to St. John recorded in the twelfth chapter of Revelation augured further coming of the impersonal Christ, Truth, in its full import. The time appointed for this sacred event arrived in the nineteenth century when the Christ Science was revealed.

Someone had to be the agent for this fulfillment of revelation; someone who would be chosen out of all the people on earth and at a time when the passing years would compel men to exchange the material sense of universe for the spiritual idea of creation. Such a consciousness would have to be prepared to listen to God, to hear and understand the wisdom of the eternal, to be able to transcribe the message for all to read, and then to substantiate what was heard by proofs of Christian healing. From the time of the awesome discovery, there could be no turning back, no faltering, no discouragement, no doubting, no evasion of divine demands, no lapse of self-requirement to measure up to duties waiting. The messenger could not stop until the journey of delivery to humanity

1

was accomplished so that Truth, forever unchanged, would be learned and lived by all men.

In the year 1866 she who is known throughout the world as Mary Baker Eddy stood at the threshold of the infinite and looked upon spiritual existence. It was not viewed as a distant possibility, but as the forever and only reality of being. Creational cause was seen to be Mind, Principle, Love, Spirit, and all that emanated from it as partaking of the divine essence and nature. The searching of matter for wisdom of Life could no longer be pursued. The pathway of understanding lay in the realm of Spirit alone. A paragraph in the textbook, "Science and Health with Key to the Scriptures" by Mrs. Eddy, graphically describes her thought: "The compounded minerals or aggregated substances composing the earth, the relations which constituent masses hold to each other, the magnitudes, distances, and revolutions of the celestial bodies, are of no real importance, when we remember that they all must give place to the spiritual fact by the translation of man and the universe back into Spirit. In proportion as this is done, man and the universe will be found harmonious and eternal." [1]

These words indicate the possession of a spiritual strength which carried her thought beyond the realm of matter and held it fixed on spirituality till the stupendous reception of divine Science was accomplished. This strength also enforced obedience of the body to spiritual law so that years of physical frailty gave way to good health; a lifetime trust in God unfolded into concrete experience of holy presence and power.

With every period of Truth's appearing to Mrs. Eddy, the seeming world of materialism grew fainter and the spiritual creation clearer until the absolute statement of the nothingness of mortality and the allness of divine existence could be declared. The functioning of Life and its infinite manifestation was seen to be divine Science. Was not this the fulfillment of the saying of Jesus that "when . . . the Spirit of truth, is come, he will guide you into all

Her fulfillment of prophecy

truth"? [2] For Science both declares and demonstrates the omnipotence of divine Principle, God.

Mrs. Eddy was nursed with Biblical prophecies and reared on them. The Scriptures stimulated in her the conviction that the time had come for the ancient words of eternal Truth to be better known as the present facts of existence. In childhood she experienced healing from a severe fever through prayer. Again she heard, as had Samuel, a sacred voice calling her and had answered, as did he, "Speak; for thy servant heareth." [3] Gradually the years brought unmistakable proofs of her conviction until she was raised from a deathbed through acceptance of the account of Jesus' healing of the palsied man told in the ninth chapter of Matthew. Thereafter unfolded the final revealment of the prophetic words of Scriptural truth as the Science of eternal Life.

The unfolding of the spiritual vision humbles the human. The magnitude and glory of divine being silence personal sense and still human ambition. This leaves no room for aught besides the hunger to know more of man in the likeness of God. The human cannot prevent the divine appearing, but is embraced in its imperative tenderness until finally yielding to Truth forever. Human humility must be in proportion to divine understanding. The Leader of Christian Science is a rare example of this truism.

Mrs. Eddy states, "In divine revelation, material and corporeal selfhood disappear, and the spiritual idea is understood." [4] She continues, "The woman in the Apocalypse symbolizes generic man, the spiritual idea of God; she illustrates the coincidence of God and man as the divine Principle and divine idea." This explanation of St. John's figure of speech gives to her who was divinely illumined to perceive it a place of impressive import in prophetic history. She touched the inner substance that had formed the holy utterances of apostles, prophets, and the master Metaphysician, Christ Jesus. She sensed the plan of Principle for its ever-enduring creation. She marveled at the beauty of man in the likeness of God.

3

This great Christian did not so much behold through effect the divine cause as the cause emitting its self-expression. Her realization started with the primary and so naturally understood the secondary. The spiritual thread out of which was woven the indestructible fabric of prophetic wisdom throughout Bible times was put in her hands that she might weave the final pattern of revelation.

The maturing concept of true womanhood appears in the last chapter of Proverbs. Isaiah beheld the achievement of womanhood's divinely bestowed purpose as recorded in the fifty-fourth chapter of his Bible record. Later St. John saw the spiritual idea of womanhood bringing forth the understanding of God, which was to rule all men with omnipotence. This sequence has continued its unfoldment until the advent of Christian Science through Mrs. Eddy's reflection of Truth. Now her works of revelation and establishment of Christian healing through a worldwide religious movement are praising her in the gates of many nations.

Lest men attribute her message to merely personal, religious fervor, Mrs. Eddy informed the world that she was a scribe under orders, adding, "And who can refrain from transcribing what God indites, and ought not that one to take the cup, drink all of it, and give thanks?" [5] What God indited could only be further fulfillment of His Word to Biblical seers, for God is changeless Truth.

There have been prophet-shepherds and kings: those who were leaders of nations and wanderers in the desert: inspired men and women. Such unique prerogative did not cease with ancient people, but persists and was exercised by Mrs. Eddy under divine direction for the sake of humanity's final progress from sense to Soul. Through her holy task the glory of God draws nearer, and its deliverance of men from every seeming form of evil goes on through scientific spiritual healing in the way the Master taught. The educated beliefs of sin and disease are losing their hold, and the gates of death cannot forever swing shut on hinges of ignorance and

Her fulfillment of prophecy

fear, but are breaking under pressure of the power of resurrection understood.

The path of fulfillment of prophecy is a rugged one, for it winds through inherited and entrenched human belief, touching the areas of superstition and education and leading ever beyond them to the realm of revelation. With the giving to the world the message of Christian Science, the laws of universal Love, came religious, medical, and philosophical opposition. Misrepresentation, criticism, and ridicule made the way harder for this lone woman. But the wonder of her pilgrimage shod her feet with strength and filled her thought with radiance. Every obstacle was overcome. She was not halted by suffering, poverty, or attempts to harm her and her work, but persisted under the shelter of divine care until her mission was completed and the world was feeling the influence of her life task.

A hundred years have passed since the promised coming of "the Spirit of truth." During this time men have been roused to the realization that God's Word needs no adjuncts of robe, ceremony, or ritual to recommend it to humanity. Within itself is the compelling vitality of awesome Truth with which to bless and heal. Christian Science relieves the concept of religion of human nonessentials and quickens it with divinity's essence. It has turned the student of the cosmos from physics to metaphysics, the sufferer from drugs to prayer, the evildoer from crime to the Love that is divine Principle. Who can measure the further glory of this resistless tide!

As God's Word continues to unfold immortality to men, it will show the scope of Mrs. Eddy's achievement. It will release the full glory of the Master's life and dispel forever the clouds of material sense. The spiritual translation of the Scriptures as given in Christian Science will transmute the earthbound concept of existence into experience of man as the son of God.

5

Mary Baker Eddy

Through her inspired illumination thrown upon the testimony of Christ Jesus and of the prophets, Mrs. Eddy takes her revered place in the forefront of the seers of the ages. Her work has formed a new epoch in the understanding and practice of the Word of God. St. John's disclosure of holy events which would embrace all nations in the divine order is being fulfilled through Christian Science. The centuries are breaking. Mankind is waking.

As the "was and is and shall be" of prophecy and fulfillment appeared to Mrs. Eddy, they illustrated not so much development of time as panorama of eternity. Of this all-embracing light, she states, "Christian Science is more than a prophet or a prophecy: it presents not words alone, but works,—the daily demonstration of Truth and Love." [6] Here is part of the glory of her contribution to Christianity, her presentation of the coincidence of divine promise and achievement. If the manifestation did not eternally exist, the message would not be true. As humanity progressively accepts infinite reality, the past, present, and future melt into the eternal now, preaching is confirmed with practice, hope reaches its goal, and faith unfolds into scientific, spiritual understanding. Prophecy and fulfillment no longer seem divorced by time but united by divine Science. "For he spake, and it was done; he commanded, and it stood fast." [7]

[1] Science and Health with Key to the Scriptures
    by Mary Baker Eddy, p. 209
[2] John 16:13
[3] I Samuel 3:10
[4] Science and Health, p. 561
[5] Miscellaneous Writings by Mary Baker Eddy, p. 311;   [6] p. 373
[7] Psalm 33:9

6

2

Mary Baker Eddy

Discoverer

by Robert Peel

A number of years ago a brilliant young biologist who was suffering from a physical and mental breakdown was given a copy of "Science and Health with Key to the Scriptures" by Mary Baker Eddy. As he read through the first chapter with a certain curiosity but little enthusiasm, he thought to himself, "This really isn't my sort of book; it simply isn't the language or the kind of ideas that make sense to me." Yet he felt himself impelled to go on reading, and before he had finished the book he was healed.

More recently a young woman in Bombay, Western-trained, with an agnostic background, was given a copy of Science and Health. Halfway down the first page of the Preface she came to the sentence, "Ignorance of God is no longer the stepping-stone to faith." [1] As she read it a wave of astonishment swept over her. "A *woman* dared to write that!" she thought. A woman had dared to challenge the agelong basis of religious faith and dogma, not in the name of agnosticism but of Christianity. She had dared to say that God could actually and demonstrably be known. At that instant the knowability of God broke on the Indian woman's educated skepticism like a light.

These are only two examples of the innumerable ways in which individuals during the past one hundred years have found Christian Science. Some have drunk it in like a thirsty traveler in the desert; some have doubted and resisted and fought their way to an acceptance of its revolutionary metaphysical propositions. But child or scholar, housewife or banker, mechanic or artist, each one who has caught even a distant glimpse of the unclouded face of Truth has shared in some small measure the experience that made Mrs. Eddy the Discoverer of Christian Science.

At the heart of that experience is the perception of a God who is infinite Love and of a creation that is infinitely lovely—free from all the ruthless tyrannies of matter, all the dread and doom of mortality. This is the vision of the kingdom of God as heralded in the New Testament; but, more than that, it is the actual experiencing of the kingdom.

Thus when in February, 1866, the allness of Spirit and the consequent unreality of matter dawned on Mrs. Eddy for the first time, that illumined moment of discovery did not leave her where she was. It lifted her from what was thought to be her deathbed into the freedom and activity of the great spiritual role she was destined to play in world history. The vision began at once to transform the very foundations of her human experience, to bring into evidence the unlimited energies and capacities of the man who was made in God's image, and to flood with light the pages of the Bible, to which she turned for a scientific understanding of the Truth that had healed her.

The moment of revelation had come to her as she was reading of one of the healings of Christ Jesus; but continued study, prayer, reasoning, spiritual growth, and practical experience were necessary over a period of years before Christian Science unfolded to her in its full amplitude and coherence. She was exploring a realm of thought where only the Founder of Christianity had been before her, and his example was never far from her thought as she diligently searched the Scriptures for the Science that underlay his life and works.

She writes: "Jesus of Nazareth was a natural and divine Scientist. He was so before the material world saw him. He who antedated Abraham, and gave the world a new date in the Christian era, was a Christian Scientist, who needed no discovery of the Science of being in order to rebuke the evidence. To one 'born of the flesh,' however, divine Science must be a discovery. Woman must give it birth." [2]

Woman is not ordinarily thought of in connection with scientific discovery, yet it is clear that her intuitive perception may reach to fundamental facts and relations of being which elude the methods of either theoretical or experimental science. Certainly spiritual-mindedness rather than brilliance of intellect must be the essential prerequisite to discovering the Science of Christianity, in which the radical logic of love produces results that confound accepted categories of thought.

It is hardly surprising that Christian Science arrived not with a fanfare of scholarship and traditional learning but with something closer to the humble though remarkable circumstances of Jesus' birth. Indeed, what Mrs. Eddy writes of Mary's conception of Jesus might equally well be said of her own discovery of Christian Science, "No advancing modes of human mind made Jesus; rather was it their subjugation, and the pure heart that sees God." [3]

Few among the sons of men might have chosen Mrs. Eddy for the revelation whose coming was to fulfill Jesus' promise that in time the Comforter, or "the Spirit of truth," would appear and guide his followers "into all truth." [4] Yet if Christian history proves anything, it proves that God's ways are not as men's ways, and the appearing of Christian Science was no exception to this rule.

What is apparent to the discerning Christian eye is that Mrs. Eddy had been uniquely fitted by her early experience to follow Jesus' command to Simon, "Launch out into the deep," [5] and to leave all halfway human positions behind her. Though endowed with an unusual love of God from her earliest years, she had been subjected to years of sternest preparation for the daring voyage into new worlds of thought that would open up to her in 1866.

11

An indispensable part of this preparation had been the stripping away of one material reliance after another: home, family, health, supply, husband, child, friends. The Christianity of her day taught that such deprivations should be accepted with meek resignation as the outcome of God's inscrutable will, but from the depths of her spiritual conviction she had rebelled against that teaching. If there was a lesson to be learned from her hardships, she would learn it—and she did, for in those years of preparation she came to see how utterly false were all hopes that rested on matter. But eagerly, persistently, importunately, she continued through her early trials to seek for the answer that she knew must lie in God's unfailing love for His creation—an answer that would enable her to conquer evil, not submit to it.

For twenty years before 1866 her search for health through various curative systems, including homeopathy and mental or magnetic healing, had educated her thought toward a perception of the mental nature of disease. Thus when the revelation of God, Spirit, as All-in-all dawned on her at her moment of crucial need, she was prepared to recognize matter as a false mode of thinking and to repudiate with the spiritual boldness of the Master himself the entire evidence of the senses.

It was no human feeling of self-sufficiency that launched Mrs. Eddy into the tempestuous waters that confronted her. Something of the nature of her experience at this time is hinted at in a single sentence, "The Discoverer of this Science could tell you of timidity, of self-distrust, of friendlessness, toil, agonies, and victories under which she needed miraculous vision to sustain her, when taking the first footsteps in this Science." [6] Without her vision of the inexhaustible and irresistible power of good, the whole enterprise would have been unthinkable.

Her actual search of the Scriptures for a full understanding of the divine Principle and rules of Christian Science was an infinitely sweet and rewarding task, as she has made plain in her writings.

12

Discoverer

As the light of revelation poured in, her heart was filled with unspeakable joy, and the healings that followed in confirmation of her findings brought with them deep assurance and encouragement.

The challenge came in communicating to the world what she was discovering, for the whole entrenched belief of life in matter seemed to concentrate itself in outraged opposition to the message and the messenger. While those who were healed were grateful and even enthusiastic, they all too often took alarm as gradually they realized the demands the new teaching made on them.

In some sense everyone who has ever glimpsed a new truth, however small or fragmentary, should be able to understand this phenomenon. An individual, for instance, finds in the unexpected compassion of a friend a new dimension of love, and this means that he has seen a little further into the real structure of the universe. Overjoyed, he undertakes to put this new insight into practice. But very soon old ways of thinking and feeling are roused to protest that he is being unrealistic, that unselfishness doesn't pay, that he'd better mind his own business and not be a do-gooder. All the self-assertive limitations of small-minded thinking seem determined to blot out what he has discovered with such delight.

The supreme example of human resistance to Truth—and of its overcoming—is found in the life of Christ Jesus. The greatest exemplar of Love the world has ever known was nailed to a cross by the hatred his example had aroused. Yet in the triumph of the resurrection he proved the ultimate powerlessness and falsity of all that opposes itself to God, as well as the indestructible reality of the Life and Love that are God. As Mrs. Eddy drank of his cup and felt the inspiration of the risen Christ in her own life, she was able to face opposition with the unshakable assurance of Truth's ultimate victory.

Very soon, however, she learned that it was not enough to have learned the nature of divine Mind's perfect creation. In order to complete and to safeguard her discovery, she must also understand

13

the workings of the carnal, or mortal, mind, described by Paul as "enmity against God." [7] Of this necessity she writes: "I shall not forget the cost of investigating, for this age, the methods and power of error. While the ways, means, and potency of Truth had flowed into my consciousness as easily as dawns the morning light and shadows flee, the metaphysical mystery of error—its hidden paths, purpose, and fruits—at first defied me. I was saying all the time, 'Come not thou into the secret'—but at length took up the research according to God's command." [8]

Her realism, as well as her determination to follow wherever Truth led, is apparent in such a passage. She writes also (see Retrospection and Introspection, pp. 37, 38) that it was not even possible for her to publish the first edition of Science and Health until she had included in it a partial explanation of what she had then discovered of the mesmeric workings of mortal mind. Honesty would not allow her to withhold any part of her discovery that might be necessary for the complete elimination of error.

Science and Health, to which in the course of several major revisions she gave its present full title "Science and Health with Key to the Scriptures," is the record of her discovery in its healing application to the grievous ills of the world. Each revision brought out more clearly the basic facts of being as she had gained them through what she describes as revelation, reason, and demonstration. The book, in its final form, is the most important single fruit of her discovery.

In the last words of the Preface she commits the pages that follow to honest seekers for Truth. She herself had been a seeker before she became a discoverer. Revelation does not come to the mentally passive, and the very title "Discoverer" points to active spiritual exploration as well as humble listening for God's guidance at every step.

The same demand is made of anyone who would understand either the discovery or the Discoverer—and the two are inseverable. Each reader of Science and Health must in a measure discover Christian Science for himself. Even a lifetime's study of the textbook will never yield up the inexhaustible riches of revelation that are there for him to discover and to demonstrate; but in order to appropriate these riches, he must be prepared to abandon cherished human positions and venture into a bracing new world where the demands of Principle are infinite—and the rewards of Love are sure.

Christian Science came through revelation, reason, and demonstration, and it needs some measure of revelation, reason, and demonstration to be understood even in part. But always as the student of Christian Science moves forward along the way Christ Jesus walked, he finds the path illumined for him by the divine Science that Mrs. Eddy labored so valiantly and devotedly to share with the world.

Each advancing step will help him to understand a little better the Christ-example that led her, the Christ-spirit that inspired her, the Christ-power that sustained her. Each deepening experience will show him a little more clearly the meaning of her words, "Bear with me the burden of discovery and share with me the bliss of seeing the risen Christ, God's spiritual idea that takes away all sin, disease, and death, and gives to soul its native freedom." [9]

[1] Science and Health, p. vii
[2] Retrospection and Introspection by Mary Baker Eddy, p. 26
[3] Miscellaneous Writings, pp. 360, 361
[4] John 16:13
[5] Luke 5:4
[6] Rudimental Divine Science by Mary Baker Eddy, p. 17
[7] Romans 8:7
[8] Miscellaneous Writings, pp. 222, 223
[9] The First Church of Christ, Scientist, and Miscellany by Mary
   Baker Eddy, p. 120

3

Founder

by Floyd C. Shank

Mary Baker Eddy—Founder! What does the word "founder" mean that it should be so closely linked with the one who has discovered Christian Science, the complete healing system of Christ Jesus? Webster's dictionary gives this meaning: "One that founds, establishes, or builds." The Founder of Christian Science, then, is the one who has immovably established Christian Science on this earth.

In the Preface to the textbook, "Science and Health with Key to the Scriptures," Mrs. Eddy discloses her divine authority for undertaking this gigantic task. She explains, "When God called the author to proclaim His Gospel to this age, there came also the charge to plant and water His vineyard." [1] How has she fulfilled this responsibility which God placed upon her? What evidence have we that she succeeded in performing a task of such magnitude? Through what avenues have her followers received directions for aiding their Leader in carrying out God's orders to her "to plant and water His vineyard"?

Evidence of her selfless obedience to this command is to be seen in the incomparable church institution which she founded and which she fostered throughout her long years of devotion to the fulfillment of God's charge. The Manual of The Mother Church by Mrs. Eddy records God's directions to her for founding an institution, the purpose of which is to forward the new birth of everyone who enters its fold by requiring obedience to Rules and

19

By-Laws which over the years were dictated to the author by divine Love.

The nameless struggle which brought her to the point where her work as Founder had to be undertaken may be glimpsed in the pathos of her words, "Until the author of this book learned the vastness of Christian Science, the fixedness of mortal illusions, and the human hatred of Truth, she cherished sanguine hopes that Christian Science would meet with immediate and universal acceptance." [2] Scriptural precedent for this rejection of the purely spiritual system of Christianity is recorded in the Gospel of John, "He came unto his own, and his own received him not." [3]

But even as the Master walked without faltering in the face of the world's hatred of Truth, so Mrs. Eddy entered unhesitatingly upon her colossal task. Facing with unwavering faith in God the magnitude of the task before her, she listened for and obeyed His guidance in healing and teaching and evolving step by step a church designed to reestablish for present and future generations Jesus' original system of the unadulterated Christ-healing.

Clifford P. Smith gives this impressive description of Mrs. Eddy's work as Founder: "As Founder, she had to find, prove, and continually supervise the appropriate modes by which to communicate her discovery, preserve its purity, and make it most beneficial to all who would accept and use it. All this she did as one divinely guided. 'And the Lord spake unto Moses face to face, as a man speaketh unto his friend' (Exodus 33:11)." [4]

How has it been possible for this lone woman to succeed in founding a vast church establishment on teachings counter to the whole current of human theories commonly accepted by the human race? The answer is in the inevitable fulfillment of Jesus' prophetic words to his disciples that he had much more to teach them than they could then comprehend. Hence his assurance that the full explanation of his method of salvation and healing

Founder

would be forthcoming at some future time. His words are, "The Comforter, which is the Holy Ghost, whom the Father will send in my name, he shall teach you all things, and bring all things to your remembrance, whatsoever I have said unto you." [5] This prophecy is now fulfilled in the lifework of Mary Baker Eddy. Through her total self-renunciation and consecration to her divine calling, the Master's complete system and its demonstration in healing have been revealed and preserved in their purity.

Thirteen years after Mrs. Eddy's discovery of Christian Science in 1866, there appeared definite evidence of her work as Founder. During those years she had demonstrated Christian Science to be Jesus' method by healing hundreds of cases of all types of disease and sin through the power of God alone; she had taught this Science to students; and she had published the textbook. Now she undertook the planting and watering of God's vineyard by organizing a church designed to reinstate primitive Christianity with its original healing element and to perpetuate in its purity her great discovery. However, after ten years of existence under a state charter, this humanly organized church was, at Mrs. Eddy's request, dissolved, although regular services were maintained.

Then on September 23, 1892, under divine guidance she established, free from the human limitations of a state charter, The First Church of Christ, Scientist, in Boston, Massachusetts—The Mother Church. On September 1 of that year, Mrs. Eddy had executed a "Deed of Trust Conveying Land for Church Edifice," stipulating that "said grantees shall be known as the 'Christian Science Board of Directors,' and shall constitute a perpetual body or corporation under and in accordance with section one, Chapter 39 of the Public Statutes of Massachusetts." [6] Thus the Founder established a legal entity for the ownership of the land and church edifices. Under this provision The Christian Science Board of Directors holds the legal title of these properties and trusts for the members of The Mother Church, and voting power is vested by the Manual in the Directors.

The Original Mother Church edifice in Boston was constructed in 1894 and was dedicated free of debt at the Sunday services, January 6, 1895. The date and the services are memorable in that it was on this occasion that the Bible and "Science and Health with Key to the Scriptures," at Mrs. Eddy's direction, became the Pastor of The Mother Church and all of its branches. In a letter addressed to The Christian Science Board of Directors, dated December 19, 1894, she made that announcement, stating in explanation that it was her intent to spiritualize thought through the pure Word, unadulterated by human views. [7]

At the Annual Meeting of The Mother Church on June 18, 1902, the thousands of members present adopted unanimously a motion to provide adequate funds for erecting the extension of The Mother Church adjoining the Original Edifice. For this action Mrs. Eddy expressed her deep and heartfelt thanks. [8] The purchase of the needed land, the completion of the new building, and payment in full for the magnificent structure enabled the opening dedicatory services to be held on June 10, 1906.

This brief summation of the Founder's progress in establishing the Cause of Christian Science, symbolized by the completion and dedication of The Mother Church edifices, is cited merely to hint at the vast growth of this new-old healing religion throughout the world. And this progress has continued during the sixty years following the dedication of The Mother Church extension. Today there are branch churches with their public Reading Rooms and also societies encircling the globe; Christian Science practitioners and teachers carrying on their healing and teaching work for humanity; and The Christian Science Publishing Society supplying the world with the religious periodicals of the Church and its daily newspaper, *The Christian Science Monitor*.

Founder

Irving C. Tomlinson makes this impressive statement: "How little the world knows, how slightly it appreciates, the hardships and the self-sacrifice of Mary Baker Eddy in presenting her inspired revelation to the sons of men! Only through divine wisdom and unceasing toil did she accomplish the work of keeping Christian Science unadulterated. What humanity owes to her foresight in establishing The Christian Science Publishing Society, it now little comprehends, but future ages will accord a just estimate to the untiring labor and manifold achievements of the Founder of the Christian Science movement." [9]

Nowhere is the vastness of Christian Science and its divinely established Church indicated more comprehensively than in the Church Manual. The deeply spiritual purpose of this Manual is outlined thus: "It stands alone, uniquely adapted to form the budding thought and hedge it about with divine Love." [10] This forming of "the budding thought" is the impelling of spiritual growth in the individual member's thought and life to the degree that the member orders his thinking and living in accord with the Manual's God-given By-Laws and Rules. In an extract from a letter in her book "Miscellaneous Writings," printed on page 3 of the Manual, Mrs. Eddy makes clear the divine origin of the Manual and its many By-Laws.

The Mother Church, with its branches, is unique. Far from being just another sect or organization, it is a divinely dictated plan for fostering and promoting the study, understanding, and demonstration of the spiritual meaning of the Scriptures as revealed in Christian Science. Does not this fact emphasize the grave responsibility resting upon each member of the Founder's Church to strive daily to increase his spiritual understanding and his obedience to the By-Laws and Rules of the Church Manual?

This complete plan can never be changed, needs never to be changed. [11] But change *must* take place in the thinking and living

23

of the members as they more and more fully comprehend and live in accord with the Tenets and By-Laws of the Church. Through obedience to the Manual, discipline of thought develops moral and spiritual power, both of which are indispensable to spiritual advancement in Christian Science.

The Founder not only has planted and watered God's vineyard, but also has provided for its perpetual care, for its continued watering and weeding and cultivating by her followers. The budding and unfolding of spiritual understanding take place in the consciousness of every member and grow to fruitage in healing disease and sin, in reformation, and in spiritual advancement. It is through our willing obedience to the Church Rules that mankind will be the beneficiary of pure Christian Science.

Is it not apparent that the purpose of our Leader's labors as Founder is to preserve the light of Truth undimmed until it reaches all mankind? In a powerful admonition Mrs. Eddy warns against any deviation from the divinely prescribed order. She says, "Guard yourselves against the subtly hidden suggestion that the Son of man will be glorified, or humanity benefited, by any deviation from the order prescribed by supernal grace." [12]

Can her followers be dismayed if at times their tasks should seem sore, when they recall the great accomplishments of the Founder as she obeyed God's call "to plant and water His vineyard"? How was she to prepare soil in which the seed of spiritual truth would grow and reach the point of fruitage? God led her step by step to comprehend and carry out His directives. Faithfully, tirelessly, she followed through success and through failures, through harmony and through discord, through poverty and through plenty!

She has given to mankind her spiritually established Church, The Mother Church, with its branches in most countries. Obviously the purpose of this Church-plan is to prepare the soil and to provide for cultivating and guarding the tender plants of spiritual

Founder

awakening as they appear above the weeds of material thinking and living.

As her followers, let us rise spiritually to study and comprehend more fully our Leader's lifework as Founder. Her Church is a prolongation of her own life purpose. It represents the Founder guiding and leading us on in our journey out of the flesh. She tells us to look for her only in her writings, which include the Church Manual. [12] Through the divinely dictated Rules and By-Laws in the Manual the Founder speaks to us with authority in behalf of her discovery. These By-Laws are the continuing means of protecting, cherishing, and mothering the true idea of God as it dawns on human thinking and living.

May we, her followers, grasp more fully the actual meaning of the Founder's stupendous work and mission, which she has fulfilled through total self-renunciation and unceasing communion with the infinite! Mrs. Eddy alone fully comprehends this. She humbly declares: "Millions may know that I am the Founder of Christian Science. I alone know what that means." [13]

[1] Science and Health, p. xi;   [2] p. 330
[3] John 1:11
[4] Historical Sketches by Clifford P. Smith, p. 64
[5] John 14:26
[6] Church Manual by Mary Baker Eddy, p. 130
[7] The Mother Church by Joseph Armstrong
[8] The First Church of Christ, Scientist, and Miscellany, pp. 7–9
[9] Twelve Years with Mary Baker Eddy by Irving C. Tomlinson, p. 111
[10] Manual, Article XXXV, Section 1;   [11] Article XXXV, Section 3
[12] Retrospection and Introspection, p. 85
[13] The First Church of Christ, Scientist, and Miscellany, p. 249

4

Mary Baker Eddy
Leader

by Ralph B. Scholfield

The discovery of Christian Science by Mary Baker Eddy and her founding of the Christian Science movement prepared her to meet the demands progressively made upon her by leadership of the Cause of Christian Science.

In course of time her teachings spread both nationally and internationally, and it became obvious that in order to preserve the accuracy and purity of her teachings a wise human control was absolutely necessary. In her Message to The Mother Church for 1900 she states: "My loyal students will tell you that for many years I have desired to step aside and to have some one take my place as leader of this mighty movement. Also that I strove earnestly to fit others for this great responsibility. But no one else has seemed equal to 'bear the burden and heat of the day.' " [1] Thus it came about that with the aid of great patience and experience she gradually stood forth in her full stature as Leader of what she herself terms "this mighty movement."

It would be difficult to say exactly when Mrs. Eddy became the publicly acknowledged Leader of the Cause of Christian Science, but there exist many records of her leadership and of her guidance given to her followers from early days. The responsibility of equipping her students for the ever-widening growth of the Christian Science movement showed her the necessity of firmly guiding and controlling both their actions and their organization. Her

29

followers needed this guidance in order to protect them from the envy, hatred, and jealousy which she and many Christian Scientists encountered from the first and which have ever been directed against spiritual growth and revelation.

In "Historical Sketches" Clifford P. Smith maintains that by 1885 Mrs. Eddy was able to demonstrate her dependable leadership and through her healing and teaching to extend the field of Christian Science beyond the limits of New England.

The rudiments of leadership are learned only by the practice of patience, justice, honesty, kindness, discipline, and wisdom. In the years leading up to this dependable leadership Mrs. Eddy gave impressive evidence of these divinely-derived qualities. Though always looking ahead for spiritual guidance and keeping the impulse to human planning within close bounds, she showed her desire to place reliance on her students. As early as 1884 she chose some of them to act as teachers of Christian Science.

By about 1887 it was becoming almost impossible for Mrs. Eddy to have any time to herself in which to think of wider plans for the promotion of Christian Science. Her correspondence, interviews, and consultations together with her teaching and writing grew to such an extent that something had to be done.

Then came her visit to the convention of the National Christian Scientist Association in Chicago in 1888. Here she received such an amazing popular reception that she knew a crisis had been reached in her work of leadership. She saw that she must lead her students into real spiritual worship as opposed to the worship of her personality. Sibyl Wilbur sums it up in this way: "Public functions and such scenes of worldly ambition had much to do with a resolve . . . to withdraw entirely from public life that the adulation of her personality might cease and the truth she taught have opportunity to make its way through the work of her students." [2]

Leader

With her move from Boston to Concord, New Hampshire, in 1889, Mrs. Eddy withdrew from the constant personal direction of her students in Boston. But this did not mean a life of seclusion. Rather did it enlarge her sphere of leadership and enable her to judge the needs of the Cause of Christian Science in its growing influence in many parts of the world. Like a general in an army, she left the immediate local details to her subordinates while she controlled the main plan of campaign on a wide front, free from importunate demands on her time and thought.

She was illustrating by her example the advice which she gives in the textbook, "Science and Health with Key to the Scriptures," to all Christian Scientists: "Christian Scientists must live under the constant pressure of the apostolic command to come out from the material world and be separate. They must renounce aggression, oppression and the pride of power. Christianity, with the crown of Love upon her brow, must be their queen of life." [3]

The spiritual greatness and power of Mrs. Eddy's leadership were now beginning to take a wider and more definite form.

The first five years of her residence in Concord gave her the opportunity of leading her church from the height of inspiration. It ultimated in the organization of The Mother Church, The First Church of Christ, Scientist, in Boston, Massachusetts, and the building of its Original Edifice. While the ground on which The Mother Church was built in 1894 was handed over to Trustees, Mrs. Eddy decided that this Church must be constituted and governed on a spiritual basis, as defined in the By-Laws of the Manual of The Mother Church, which she wrote. And through her wisdom and foresight this is where it stands today.

On February 27, 1903, in a letter addressed to The Christian Science Board of Directors and placed in the records of The Mother Church, Mrs. Eddy gave this definite order: "Never abandon the By-laws nor the denominational government of the Mother

Church." [4] The Mother Church exists, therefore, to guide and control through the Manual the Cause of Christian Science. By this procedure Mrs. Eddy freed it from human interference. Of her leadership through this period, Sibyl Wilbur writes: "In doing this she succeeded in withdrawing her own personality from the clashing world of events, leaving only Truth enthroned for ruler. What wonder that her devoted followers lovingly call her Leader!" [5]

From this point we see Mrs. Eddy's leadership manifested largely in adding new By-Laws to the Manual or amending some of the old ones; also in writing letters or messages of advice, encouragement, and constructive criticism to The Mother Church, to many branch churches, and to individuals. At the same time she kept always in close touch with the Board of Directors in Boston.

Something had to be done to protect the Church from the widespread preaching and doctrines that were not in accord with Christian Science. In her first message to The Mother Church in 1895, [6] Mrs. Eddy began by implying that spiritual food was to be sought and found in a knowledge of the Scriptures and in the correlative passages in her textbook. Her institution of the *Christian Science Quarterly* Bible Lessons ensured that no personal preaching should take place in Christian Science services. To cover this, she decreed that the Bible and Science and Health were to be Pastor over The Mother Church—The First Church of Christ, Scientist, in Boston, Massachusetts—and provided that they should forever continue to preach. [7] She made it clear that the prosperity of the Christian Science Cause depended largely on these Lesson-Sermons. [8]

She also ruled concerning the individual member, "The BIBLE, together with SCIENCE AND HEALTH and other works by Mrs. Eddy, shall be his only textbooks for self-instruction in Christian Science, and for teaching and practising metaphysical healing." [9]

Leader

Mrs. Eddy's early experience with those who attempted to plagiarize her writings or who thought that their vision was in advance of hers would alone have been sufficient to make this strict By-Law necessary. While she did not discourage the reading of good literature, her emphasis on obtaining self-instruction in Christian Science from only one source was an instance of her wise leadership. She also gave orders that in Christian Science Reading Rooms only her writings and literature sold or published by The Christian Science Publishing Society were to be available. [10]

Mrs. Eddy expressed a very great love for and appreciation of the Bible. It could truly be said that it was the spiritual interpretation of the Scriptures that led her and showed her how to lead her Church. Her orders could well be summed up in the words of Paul: "Put on the whole armour of God, that ye may be able to stand against the wiles of the devil. . . . And take . . . the sword of the Spirit, which is the word of God." [11]

No important activity in the Christian Science movement is without some wise and specific instruction from her as a basis for action. In this she has shown no narrowness of vision or attempt to dominate, but has demanded strict compliance with the spirit of the Scriptures and the textbook. To give only a few examples of her leadership, she safeguarded the practice of teaching Christian Science by definite Rules. She gave instructions for the appointment of Christian Science lecturers. She made simple but clear regulations for the formation of branch churches and societies and for their democratic government. She laid down the rules for the holding of church services and for the teaching in Christian Science Sunday Schools. In the Manual she enjoined her followers to prove that Christian Science heals the sick quickly and wholly, and she has given them at least three definite admonitions to be observed daily, whereby they may acknowledge and prove the power of Spirit over matter and good over evil.

Mrs. Eddy's writings contain many specific messages of comfort and guidance both to branch churches and to individuals. The following is part of a letter to a church many hundred miles from Boston. It is the writing of a true Leader and friend. "You whose labors are doing so much to benefit mankind will not be impatient if you have not accomplished all you desire, nor will you be long in doing more." [12] She adds, "Over sea and over land, Christian Science unites its true followers in one Principle, divine Love, that sacred *ave* and essence of Soul which makes them one in Christ."

With the Cause of Christian Science reaching more and more to many parts of the world, toward the turn of the century Christian Science was in a measure passing from a stage of persecution to a phase of popularity.

Mrs. Eddy decided in 1898 to supply this growing public interest with a weekly paper to supplement *The Christian Science Journal* founded by her in 1883 and published monthly. She wished to have accurate statements of Christian Science teaching and healing reach inquirers more frequently. And thus she brought out the *Christian Science Sentinel,* a weekly. This she followed five years later, in 1903, with *The Herald of Christian Science,* at first published in German (with English interleaved) but now appearing in many additional languages (with English interleaved) and Braille. She ensured by certain rules that The Christian Science Publishing Society should have the responsibility of issuing only literature that is correct in its statement of Christian Science.

Mrs. Eddy was herself a constant contributor to her periodicals. Through them she issued not only new Rules for the Church Manual, but many letters of encouragement, guidance, and even warning to the Field. She kept a close scrutiny on these periodicals, both criticizing and correcting where necessary, but often expressing commendation and praise.

An extract from one of Mrs. Eddy's directives to the editor of the periodicals reads: "Healing is the best sermon, healing is the best lecture, and the entire demonstration of Christian Science. The sinner and the sick healed are our best witnesses." [13]

In 1908 Mrs. Eddy left Concord to return to Boston where she completed the crowning event of her leadership. This was the establishing of the daily newspaper *The Christian Science Monitor*. All through her experience she took a most lively and intelligent interest in both national and international affairs, many of which are alluded to in her writings. She knew that with a daily newspaper she could set the world an example of how to check the unceasing journalistic propaganda which dwelt on and suggested so much misery and discord. She saw too the opportunity of helping her followers, and all people looking for higher moral and ethical standards, to learn more of the infinite power of good over evil.

In July, 1908, Mrs. Eddy wrote to the Board of Directors: "So soon as the Pub. House debt is paid I request The C. S. Board of Directors to start a daily newspaper called *Christian Science Monitor*. This must be *done* without fail." [14] Before the paper was launched Mrs. Eddy had to deal with many objections and obstacles to her plans. One of these was the desire on the part of some of her students to omit the words "Christian Science" from the title of the paper. After consulting with Mrs. Eddy, the editor reported, "Mrs. Eddy is firm, and her answer is, 'God gave me this name and it remains.' " [15] Thereby she definitely associated Christian Science with clean journalism.

Mrs. Eddy's greatness lay in her unswerving spiritual leadership. Through the textbook and her other writings she still leads and speaks to her followers and to all mankind.

Although leading a vital religious movement herself, she strongly recommended and even ordered her followers to show full sympathy, kindness, and charity to all differing forms of religion and medicine. But her leadership had as its main purpose the reintroduction of the spirit and power of Christian or spiritual healing and regeneration through prayer, as taught and practiced by Christ

Jesus. A knowledge, appreciation, and love of their Leader are indispensable to all Christian Scientists, together with an understanding of her place in the history of Christian religion.

Irving C. Tomlinson writes, "The fruits of her life are seen in regenerated lives; in lives brought back from the brink of the grave, saved from the ravages of consuming fears, redeemed from degrading sin and want and misery; in hearts comforted and healed of consuming grief; in lives raised from deepest darkness to the light of renewed hope and joy and courage." [16] Truly the Biblical words, "By their fruits ye shall know them," [17] are applicable to the spiritual life and leadership of Mary Baker Eddy.

[1] Message to The Mother Church for 1900 by Mary Baker Eddy, p. 9
[2] The Life of Mary Baker Eddy by Sibyl Wilbur, p. 311
[3] Science and Health, p. 451
[4] Mary Baker Eddy: A Life Size Portrait by Lyman P. Powell, 1950 Edition, p. 193
[5] The Life of Mary Baker Eddy, p. 331
[6] Miscellaneous Writings, pp. 106–110
[7] Manual, Art. XIV, Sect. 1; [8] Art. III, Sect. 1; [9] Art. IV, Sect. 1;
[10] Art. XXI, Sect. 3
[11] Ephesians 6:11, 17
[12] The First Church of Christ, Scientist, and Miscellany, pp. 203, 204
[13] *The Christian Science Journal,* May, 1936
[14] Commitment to Freedom by Erwin D. Canham, p. 22
[15] Twelve Years with Mary Baker Eddy, p. 106; [16] p. 208
[17] Matthew 7:20

5

Mary Baker Eddy

Lecturer and preacher

by Paul Stark Seeley

Rays of spiritual, eternal truth have been breaking through the mist of material ignorance for unnumbered centuries. This timeless dawn of spiritual reality was evidenced in the thinking of Melchizedek and Abraham, followed by the great Bible characters through whose Spirit-enlightened thinking appeared the Word of God recorded in the Old Testament. Since spiritual foresight accompanies spiritual enlightenment, it was inevitable that the prophets should discern events to come that were essential to the fulfillment of the divine purpose, that all material ignorance be destroyed by the God-impelled light of divine intelligence in such human ways as mankind could recognize and understand.

Micah and Zechariah foresaw that two messengers would appear to further and fulfill this divine purpose. The first, Christ Jesus, by the spoken word and mighty proofs of the healing power of God's Word defined the basic issue between good and evil to be between the forces of deific Mind and the forces of the godless, lying evil mind, objectified in mutable mortal man and perishable things. That the divine purpose demanded a subsequent revelation of truth the Master made clear in these prophetic words: "I will pray the Father, and he shall give you another Comforter, that he may abide with you for ever." [1] John, in the twelfth chapter of Revelation, reiterates Micah's prophecy that she who travaileth shall bring forth that revelation of eternal truth which shall rule all peoples.

Mary Baker Eddy:

This second appearing of revealed truth was made available to humanity in 1875 with the publishing of Science and Health by Mary Baker Eddy. It appeared nine years after she had been expected to die from an accident and was restored to health through her unfaltering trust in the healing might of deific Mind. She was then living at Swampscott, near Lynn, Massachusetts, on the Atlantic seacoast about ten miles north of Boston. Immediately following her healing she devoted several years to deep research into the Bible to gain a demonstrable knowledge of the basic rules and laws of eternal Mind for applying its healing power to human needs. Science and Health contains her conclusions. Of the origin of this book, she writes, "It was not myself, but the divine power of Truth and Love, infinitely above me, which dictated 'Science and Health with Key to the Scriptures.' " [2]

With her great discovery of God's immanent healing power came responsibility. Mrs. Eddy recognized that what divine Mind had revealed to her was to be given by her to mankind. In Science and Health she says, "When God called the author to proclaim His Gospel to this age, there came also the charge to plant and water His vineyard." [3]

How to accomplish this in a world loath to forsake its manmade creeds and theological dogmas and its long-educated reliance on material remedies rather than on God for healing was no simple task. But the consciousness which had been able to feel and demonstrate God's healing power knew that the source which had given her this light would wisely guide her every step for firmly founding in human thought the spiritual idea of being which constituted her discovery.

Ways to communicate the message of Christian Science to mankind must be found by her and utilized. Men were not willing to buy Science and Health simply because of her faith in its message. The public must be awakened to consider the timeless verities of spiritual being and their practical applicability to the everyday needs of men. Mrs. Eddy alone was, then, able to do this.

40

Lecturer and preacher

Of all the people on earth Mrs. Eddy only had then found and proven men's God-given ability to understand and demonstrate the healing might of Mind to be the same as Jesus had proved it to be. No fear that she might not be able to fulfill her mission was tolerated.

Soon after her healing in February, 1866, she began to share the good news with those who showed interest in her discovery. During the next winter she accepted her first student. Gradually others desired to be taught. By 1875 there were enough persons interested to start services which Mrs. Eddy conducted in a hall in Lynn, where she was then living. These usually included a sermon by Mrs. Eddy. Her public presentation of Christian Science through the spoken word had now begun. Though the fruitage was at first meager, the good seed was being sown and was taking root. The Comforter's message of God's healing power was being recognized.

Through friends and students, group meetings were arranged in homes in some Boston suburbs, and here she gave many talks on Christian Science which she called parlor lectures. In 1875, the year Science and Health appeared, she asked for and received a letter of dismissal from the Congregational Church, of which she had been a member for thirty-seven years.

The lectures to small groups and her conducting of services in Lynn enabled her to reach more and more people with her healing message. But the small attendance at the services—at most one hundred and usually much fewer—showed Mrs. Eddy that a larger field of activity must be found for this word of truth. After giving many parlor lectures, she made it known that she felt she must reach greater numbers and a larger field.

Three years after the publication of Science and Health she began to deliver public lectures, or sermons, in Boston. First, she filled the pulpit in the Baptist Tabernacle, whose pastor had been unable to hold the interest of its members. During the four months she preached there, the attendance so increased that the pews were too few to hold the people, and benches were brought in. Then she preached at Parker Memorial Hall in Boston for several months and was given a warm welcome, many being healed by her sermons. Thirty-two lectures were given by her in Boston between November, 1878, and July, 1879.

In April, 1879, the Church of Christ, Scientist, was born with fourteen or fifteen members present. Then, in November, 1881, Mrs. Eddy was formally ordained its Pastor. It was the official beginning of her status first as Pastor and later as Pastor Emeritus.

She once felt she should lecture in a neighboring town and wrote a student there to make the arrangements, urging her to see that the lecture was well heralded and saying that handbills should be used. She emphasized the need for getting out numbers.

For the most part, Mrs. Eddy's lectures and sermons were received cordially and aroused keen interest which resulted in increased sales of Science and Health. She thoroughly enjoyed answering questions that were asked at the close of a lecture. On one occasion when a minister attempted to cut off her time for replies, the audience, by stamping and applauding, demanded time be given her, and it was. On another occasion the enthusiasm of a large audience in Boston required an hour for her to shake hands with those who desired to express their gratitude. In a single week she gave eight lectures in addition to her interviews with inquirers and patients.

As a public speaker Mrs. Eddy realized that divine Mind was using her to sow the good seed of Truth's Word. She was able so to impart her message that it did not become shadowed by her personality. Her natural dignity, poise, and conviction as to the truth she was voicing left an enduring impression on her hearers. The Christian Scientists who heard her were made to feel a great Cause needed to be established, and they were needed for it.

As the months passed, requests were coming in from various cities for her to lecture. In 1882, in addition to speaking in Boston,

Lecturer and preacher

she lectured on Christian Science in the nation's capital, Washington, District of Columbia. From its sturdy New England cradle, this new-old message was finding its way to receptive hearts in an ever-widening field. The universality of its appeal was beginning to be realized.

As Truth's messenger must be of Truth's choosing, so the place for the appearing of Truth's message could be no matter of chance. As Christ Jesus appeared where his holy message could receive some measure of recognition and be recorded for future ages, so the Comforter came to that part of the New World where its message of divine healing was assured a fair opportunity to be recognized and to take root.

Mrs. Eddy was God-equipped with the courage, fearlessness, inspiration, and patience to start with the spoken word to communicate the revelation of the Christ Science, or Comforter, to mankind. The years immediately following her discovery made an imperative demand on her for action. She responded with her whole heart. In the first ten years she found individuals and groups close by her who were ready to listen to the truths the divine Mind had revealed to her. This was the planting time.

In the second ten years fruitage appeared from the seed already planted, and spontaneous requests for public lectures over an ever-increasing area were received. A vital step in founding Christian Science in human consciousness had been successfully taken because Mrs. Eddy had proven herself willing and able to become the first thoroughly equipped lecturer since Christ Jesus and Paul to expound the Science of Christ.

In 1889 Mrs. Eddy moved from Boston, where she had come to live in 1882, to a life of busy quietude in Concord, New Hampshire, some seventy-five miles from Boston. After making this move, she seldom spoke from the public platform except on the few occasions when she addressed her Church. Her call to preach and lecture was to serve the need of her Cause during the early years of its inception. She now had many other demands to fill, growing out of a rapidly expanding church organization.

Mindful of the highly successful pioneer work she had done from the public platform for the Cause of Christian Science, she established in 1898 The Christian Science Board of Lectureship. It carries forward the work she so wisely initiated to obey the Founder of Christianity, "Go ye into all the world, and preach the gospel to every creature." [4]

Christ Jesus, the first of Truth's great messengers to mankind, foretold by the prophets, spake to men as no man had ever spoken. It was his understanding of man's unity with the Father Mind that enabled him to be the messenger to speak God's Word to men. Said he, "As the Father said unto me, so I speak." [5] His words were nothing less than the eternally omnipresent, deific Mind audibly communicating its thoughts to men. Jesus tells us, "The words that I speak unto you, they are spirit, and they are life." [6]

Mrs. Eddy, who had made his teachings her own, through years of study, prayer, and self-immolation, became qualified to be the subsequent messenger of Truth, foreseen by the prophets, to complete Truth's revelation by defining the wisdom-revealed rules for its application to the solution of all human needs.

From the time Mrs. Eddy proved in 1866 the present availability of God's healing power, she realized that her discovery was of God's giving and that its objective was to dissolve material ignorance with the thought-forces of divine intelligence. Through her Mind-enlightened consciousness came the revealed truth that constitutes Science and Health and provides the key to the spiritual meaning of the Scriptures.

As in Jesus' time, so today the spoken word of Truth is indispensable to arousing human thought to discern the oncoming dawn of spiritual reality. By her lectures in private homes, by her sermons in her own church and other churches, and by her lectures from the public platform in receptive city areas, Mrs. Eddy proved

Lecturer and preacher

that she sufficiently understood man's unity with the all-knowing Mind that is God, to speak His Word with healing power and lasting blessings for mankind.

Hers was the God-ordered mission—symbolized in Revelation as a woman clothed with the sun, the radiance of spiritual truth—inspired by deific Mind to proclaim the message which, Christ Jesus said, "will guide you into all truth." [7]

During the past century Jesus' prophecy of the coming of the Comforter, the spirit of Truth, has been fulfilled. Its teaching has enabled its students to prove the immanence of the healing might of the forces of the basic intelligent Mind that is the one God.

The Comforter is presently here, proving that the greatest of physicians spoke with scientific accuracy when in twelve simple words he gave this recipe for the healing of all discord and disease: "Ye shall know the truth, and the truth shall make you free." [8]

[1] John 14:16
[2] The First Church of Christ, Scientist, and Miscellany, p. 114
[3] Science and Health, p. xi
[4] Mark 16:15
[5] John 12:50;   [6] 6:63;   [7] 16:13;   [8] 8:32

6

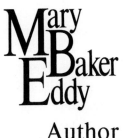

Mary Baker Eddy

Author

by Peter J. Henniker–Heaton

Monthly on the cover of *The Christian Science Journal* Mary Baker Eddy is named as author of the Christian Science textbook, "Science and Health with Key to the Scriptures." To many Mrs. Eddy is known as the Discoverer and Founder of Christian Science, the beloved Leader and organizer of an active religious movement. But to many others she is first an author, and specifically author of Science and Health.

The latter have reason so to think of her. In a moment of emptiness or grief, of physical despair or moral vertigo, they have come upon this book and read it. Grief has lifted; frustration has made way for new purpose; moral balance has been regained; disease, sometimes inveterate, organic, medically judged incurable, has been healed, completely and permanently.

This healing virtue found in Science and Health is basic to all of Mrs. Eddy's writings on Christian Science. Any evaluation of her as author must give it full weight. Science and Health first appeared in 1875. Since 1902 all its editions have included one hundred pages of testimonies from men and women right across the United States, in the provinces of Canada, and in the United Kingdom; these, selected from many thousands available, tell of lives transformed by the reading of Science and Health. The various Christian Science periodicals too from their earliest issues have carried similar testimonies; they still carry such from all around the globe. The written word from Mrs. Eddy's pen expounds, challenges, and persuades. It also heals. It changes phenomena. It exercises power.

The Bible recognizes repeatedly that "the word of God is quick, and powerful," [1] precisely accomplishing God's purposes. The Bible exercises power because it contains God's Word. This Word appears progressively in the sayings and experiences of patriarchs, prophets, and finally of Christ Jesus; in him "the Word was made flesh," [2] God's Word was expressed in terms of a human life.

Mrs. Eddy's healing in 1866, from which she dates her discovery of Christian Science, came as she read the Bible. The Swiss theologian Karl Barth has written: "It is not the right human thoughts about God which form the content of the Bible, but the right divine thoughts about men. The Bible tells us not how we should talk with God but what He says to us." The Bible has exercised transforming power upon men's lives, because its content came by divine inspiration and impulsion. Its writers record the Word of God.

The truths of Science and Health came to Mrs. Eddy by this same divine impulsion. The stupendous revelation of Christian Science dawned on her thought with shining irresistible certainty; and she found corroboration for it in the Bible. The Scriptures had been her lifelong companion. Now for three years following her healing they were virtually her sole reading. A few years after the earliest publication of her book, then called "Science and Health," she added to the title "with a Key to the Scriptures." (Later the "a" was dropped.) From the first she had intended it to be this key. Her revelation was to unlock for readers the springs of Scriptural power.

Mrs. Eddy's writings heal because, like the Bible, they contain the Word of God. Science and Health is not the speculations of an enlightened human thought about God. It is an inspired record

Author

of what God says of Himself, His own declaration of His will and purpose and ability to bless. Here the divine Word is expressed not through personal life-histories but as universal Science; once again the Word is "made flesh" but now in the form of Christ-healing.

Of the Christian Science textbook, Mrs. Eddy writes simply, "It was not myself, but the divine power of Truth and Love, infinitely above me, which dictated 'Science and Health with Key to the Scriptures.' " [3] Of her writings on Christian Science in general she says, "I was a scribe under orders." [4] To those who have found healing in her writings, these statements make sense; they carry conviction.

Inspired writing is not easy writing. It is not automatic writing. It does not bypass individuality. In the Bible, God's Word expressed itself through individuals. And it made mighty demands on them. They must let go all sense of personal selfhood, personal ability, personal achievement; yet they must harness to God's service whatever they already had of talent, training, experience, diligence, uniqueness. Divinely impelled, Mrs. Eddy, like the Bible writers, responded to this twofold demand, humanly contradictory but divinely normal.

What did Mrs. Eddy bring to her task of inspired authorship? What demand did it make upon her? How was she able to respond so totally to the demand?

From childhood she aspired to write a book. She studied to equip herself with a general background of knowledge. She read. She cultivated an excellent memory. Her abundant sympathies and ready interest brought intellectual and emotional enrichment. By her mid-twenties she was regularly contributing to various New England publications. Her output included verse and romantic fiction. She also wrote directly on political and social matters, morals and religion.

Mrs. Eddy's discovery of Christian Science gave her literary development new orientation. To write a book was no longer a

51

human aspiration; it was divine necessity. It is easy to overrate the importance of Mrs. Eddy's earlier experience of authorship. In founding Christian Science she successfully discharged heavy tasks for which she had had no human preparation. To one called upon to develop new skills in a related area, prior professional training can actually prove a hindrance. But at least Mrs. Eddy knew the labors of authorship. The word "leisure" appears nowhere in her books. She was ready to work tirelessly—revising, clarifying, purifying—so that the Word of God might shine out unobscured.

In an early sermon Mrs. Eddy states, "God is All, and in all: that finishes the question of a good and a bad side to existence." [5] This for her was no philosophic abstraction. She ends the same paragraph: "If you wish to be happy, argue with yourself on the side of happiness; take the side you wish to carry, and be careful not to talk on both sides, or to argue stronger for sorrow than for joy. You are the attorney for the case, and will win or lose according to your plea."

These seventy-four words, sixty of them with only one syllable, give the core of Mrs. Eddy's discovery: that God, good, is All, that evil is consequently nothing, and that these truths are progressively provable in human experience. She had searched the Scriptures for the Christly law behind Jesus' works. She had found it. She had made the greatest spiritually scientific breakthrough since Jesus' time. It was, indeed, the final breakthrough; there can be nothing beyond the fact that good is all, that evil is nothing, and that this allness and nothingness are scientifically demonstrable. Upon this courageous solitary penetration of unmapped mental territory Mrs. Eddy had now to report.

Communicating a discovery is a problem even to the natural scientist. In 1895 Roentgen discovered a new type of ray. The next year *The Christian Science Journal* reprinted this contemporary comment: "There is as yet no name for the interesting

Author

stranger." This "stranger" is still known as an X ray, X denoting an unknown quantity.

Similar, but immensely more complex, was the problem Mrs. Eddy faced. She must communicate utterly new spiritual truths in language formed primarily to serve humanity's material wants. How triumphantly she mastered this problem is witnessed by the fruitage from her writings. The spiritually hungry, whatever their human background, have responded to these. Men, women, quite young children, have drawn from them spiritual comfort, healing, direction, and a deep concern to share the good news with others.

To convey her thought, Mrs. Eddy sometimes picked a striking term from the speech of her day. Seeing the downward drag exerted on deluded mortals by the animal lie of sentient matter, she identified "animal magnetism" as exactly fitted to specify the nature and action of this suppositional opposite of divine Truth. Oftener she chose ordinary words, irradiating them with new spiritual light.

Justice Oliver Wendell Holmes, delivering a Supreme Court opinion, once said, "A word . . . is the skin of a living thought and may vary greatly in color and content according to the circumstances and the time in which it is used." Mrs. Eddy frequently employs a single word for divergent purposes according to context. Her language is accurate but dynamic. It discourages any illusion that spiritual revelation can be snared in rigid verbal formulas. More familiar with Webster than with the Oxford-style dictionary, she makes current developing usage, not ancient roots, the prime factor in her choice of words; on occasion she contributes to their development herself.

In spiritual teaching, metaphors and similar figures of speech play an essential part in bridging the chasm between human appearance and divine actuality. In her autobiographical sketch, "Retrospection and Introspection," Mrs. Eddy mentions, "From childhood I was a verse-maker." [6] As such she had long experience with metaphor, simile, and symbol. Her metaphors drawn from optics and astronomy provide but two examples of her skill in this area of language.

Even a passing literary fashion, employed by Mrs. Eddy, transcends conventionality; she clothes it in lasting significance. "Dear reader," she writes, and "dear sufferer." Divine Love, which she had discovered to be the Principle of the universe, is infinitely adaptable; her statement of its law and operation addresses itself to each reader, each sufferer, at the point of his need at the moment of reading. So daily, decade after decade, individuals turn to Science and Health and find its pages as though written specifically for them, as though written for that very hour.

Christian Science, being Science, can be taught. Science and Health is a textbook. Among its roots were notes which Mrs. Eddy made for teaching; and she expected her students to use it for teaching. In preparing new editions, she sometimes engaged literary assistants; these worked under her close supervision. In 1901 two such helpers received written instructions that read in part, "First be sure that you gain my meaning, and then preserve it strictly throughout the book." [7] One of them later wrote, "The book has improved, and it is because *she* has improved it." [8] Science and Health remains a textbook for teacher and student; today, within the terms of this primary purpose, it is also a work of literature.

Some of these matters may seem only the small change of authorship. But it is as many small problems are patiently and faithfully solved by authors that great seminal books come into being to fling their potent seed across the ages, as Science and Health has already begun to do.

Mrs. Eddy's published writings on Christian Science include books, sermons, articles, poems, and the Manual of The Mother Church. One who knew her well has written: "The other writings of Mary Baker Eddy . . . seem to me to be the records of her

Author

own demonstration of Science and Health. They are the breaking of the bread of Life contained in the textbook, and are inspired by the same divine Spirit." [9] Those who have been touched by the healing power of these other writings have no doubt of their inspiration.

The scenes where Mrs. Eddy wrote or meditated—the little houses at Amesbury and Stoughton, her attic room at Lynn with skylight and rocker, Red Rock, wave-lapped and fanned by ocean breezes, and her last more spacious home at Chestnut Hill—may be visited. They have their interest. But the one constant topographical feature in Mrs. Eddy's authorship is altitude, the spiritual altitude of her healing thought. From this peak of unselfed love for God and men, of moral purity and far-ranging vision, she listened for the divine word and recorded it. Guided by Spirit, she found problems of language and communication solved.

"Christian Science," Mrs. Eddy writes, "involves a new language, and a higher demonstration of medicine and religion. It is the 'new tongue' of Truth, having its best interpretation in the power of Christianity to heal." [10] Readers may assess Mrs. Eddy's writings by various standards; each one's judgment is largely a measure of his own spiritual qualifications or lack of them. Whoever responds to the spiritual power in her books is healed and blessed. By such the magnitude of Mrs. Eddy's achievement as an author is understood. By such, in reverence, gratitude, and love, it is correctly evaluated.

[1] Hebrews 4:12
[2] John 1:14
[3] The First Church of Christ, Scientist, and Miscellany, p. 114
[4] Miscellaneous Writings, p. 311
[5] Christian Healing by Mary Baker Eddy, p. 10
[6] Retrospection and Introspection, p. 11
[7] Historical Sketches, p. 108;   [8] p. 109
[9] We Knew Mary Baker Eddy, First Series, p. 47
[10] No and Yes by Mary Baker Eddy, p. 44

7

Mary Baker Eddy

Practitioner

by Elizabeth Glass Barlow

The names Mary Baker Eddy and Christian Science are indissolubly woven in the annals of history. To think of either of them is to think of healing.

Christian Science was ushered in with healing. Mrs. Eddy's own remarkable healing, wrought of God alone when she was suffering from serious injuries, resulted in the discovery of Christian Science. This healing, which occurred as the Scriptures were illumined, came so quietly, so gently, the world scarcely noticed. Later mankind was to marvel and to see the effects of her healing and teaching reach the corners of the earth.

The tremendous revelation of the allness of God and the scientific nothingness of mortal mind and matter—the powerlessness of evil to defeat God's holy purpose—had unfolded to her. This, she knew, was Christ's Science, God's unerring law, which is destined to lift the burden of mortality from the shoulders of mankind—the Science as almighty in demonstration as when Christ Jesus lived and proved its truths almost two thousand years ago.

In her autobiography, "Retrospection and Introspection," she tells how her discovery brought the radiance of divine Love to everything she beheld. And then she adds, "Frozen fountains were unsealed." [1] As we ponder her mission and the heights to which it took her, we see that her healing works were constantly unsealing the world's frozen resistance to Truth, melting the hardened concepts of the carnal mind's fear and incredulity and revealing the man of God's creating full-blown in beauty and holiness. The presence of God was to her a living fact. She writes in the Christian Science textbook, "Science and Health with Key to the Scriptures," "The evidence of divine Mind's healing power and absolute control is to me as certain as the evidence of my own existence." [2]

In the magnitude of her spiritual healing Mrs. Eddy stands alone in this age. Her work shone with the resplendence of divine Love. To her, sonship was untarnished by mortality. She saw man as the Father has created him, wearing the robes of righteousness, and on these robes there are no stains of sin or earthiness.

Christ Jesus stood as her shining example. Throughout her life was threaded the prayer to understand him better and to do the healing works he promised his followers would do. "The Son can do nothing of himself," he declared, "but what he seeth the Father do: for what things soever he doeth, these also doeth the Son likewise." [3] She recognized his marvelous vision in seeing God as the All-power. Reverently she writes of this scientific seeing: "Jesus beheld in Science the perfect man, who appeared to him where sinning mortal man appears to mortals. In this perfect man the Saviour saw God's own likeness, and this correct view of man healed the sick." [4]

And now in 1866 this healing had come to her. The words of Peter and John as they stood before the tribunal in Jerusalem may well have echoed in her thought, "We cannot but speak the things which we have seen and heard." [5] She too had been commissioned of God to speak.

But how could she make mankind hear, how could she make them understand, this lone woman, this only Christian Scientist on the earth? Not by human means. She was sure of this. In the mighty work that lay before her there could be neither trust in nor dependence upon human means. The human must yield to the divine. Divinity must reveal itself; this alone could show her the way. In selfless love and communion with God she prayed— and listened. Then in clearest terms her direction came from the Father: "Healing!"

This was her answer. This is what mankind would understand. This they would want. Just as Christ Jesus sent his disciples forth to heal, so the command from the Christ came to this disciple to heal. In faithful obedience she started out to offer healing to anyone who would listen. She did not offer treatment. She offered healing. Many were healed. And some stayed to learn the theology of this healing, so different from anything they had heard before, a theology that would transform their lives. They were familiar with the scholastic teaching which says God and man have been separated by "original sin," by a remote mortal named Adam.

But here from the lips and pen of this woman they learned of a God who is Love—of perfect God and perfect man, a great First Cause and a radiant effect called man and the universe, ever distinct but never divorced. In Mrs. Eddy's continuing spiritual awareness no belief of a broken relationship dimmed her vision of the oneness of God and man. It is this oneness, or unity, she knew, that is evil's surest annihilation. She never left her inspired standpoint of looking out from the understanding of God, Mind, to see correctly the one and only creation.

In the life of Mrs. Eddy, healing was not a robe to be donned on certain occasions when uplifting or helping someone in distress. It was an uninterrupted awareness of Immanuel, or "God with us," present in the minutest detail of her everyday living.

In the *Christian Science Sentinel* of July 18, 1908, we read of a man who was badly crippled. He could no nothing for himself but was dependent upon his brother, with whom he lived, to take entire care of him. On pleasant days a special policeman was engaged to wheel him out on Boston Common for an airing. One day as he sat there in his chair Mrs. Eddy passed by. She stopped and talked a moment with him about God. When the man was taken home he insisted that Mrs. Eddy had helped him. For days after that when he was on the Common he waited and hoped for her coming again.

She did come, and again she stopped and told him of the Christ. After this talk he was healed. His niece, in writing of this to Mrs. Eddy, said that her uncle's legs were straightened and that he was restored to complete health. He was able to establish himself in business and become self-supporting. The niece concluded her letter with these words: "It was you, dear Leader, who spoke to him of the healing Christ and set him free."

What depths of holiness must Mrs. Eddy have seen as she looked at this man! What glory of ever-present Love must she have beheld to have so changed and renewed a life! The purity of her own thought and vision revealed what was actually present —not a crippled mortal who needed to be healed, but man, made in the image and likeness of God.

As she walked across the park that day, how easy it might have been to have ignored this crippled man, this stranger. But no. With Mrs. Eddy it was the Christ-spirit at every point, the outpouring love, the healing touch. To her, realization and demonstration were one, not the demonstration trailing the realization but Mind and manifestation, simultaneous and coexistent.

There was neither dualism nor doubt in the work of this great woman. With authority she wielded the sword of the Spirit, the understanding of Truth, which is far more effective than the knife of the surgeon. In her book "Unity of Good" she tells of healing instantaneously a cancer which had eaten its way to the jugular vein. And she reveals the secret of this healing power by saying

Practitioner

"that an acknowledgment of the perfection of the infinite Unseen confers a power nothing else can." [6]

Where could one find teachers more radical and absolute than Jesus of Nazareth and Mary Baker Eddy? Yet neither of them disregarded what appeared as the human need. The hungry were fed, the sick healed. Their work was specific and pointed. There is nothing vague or abstract about scientific healing. At one time, after healing a case of dumbness and deafness, Jesus said, "If I with the finger of God cast out devils, no doubt the kingdom of God is come upon you." [7] In like manner the work of Mrs. Eddy illustrated "the finger of God," the pointed, focused, unscattered activity of divine Love operative as Christian Science treatment.

What does healing mean? Not merely relief from physical difficulties. Divinely wrought, it means a new birth. In a certain sense healing indicates the necessity of Love to express itself. It is God made manifest here and now, showing forth the order, health, certainty, and holiness which constitute true identity. Nor can it be left there. One must, as Mrs. Eddy did, bring out these facts in daily experience, in hourly living. This healing is not achieved by careless or flippant repetition of words, by dilatory methods, or by thoughtless leaning upon others. It demands the deepest humility and consecration, a willingness to put off the self-centered view of oneself and one's universe.

Mrs. Eddy has removed from healing the swaddling clothes and winding sheet of materialistic methods. Because of her spiritual greatness and the revelation she has given to the world, healing now shines forth in its full and scientific meaning, free from material theories, unmixed with medical techniques.

She dared to challenge the depths of the carnal mind's subtlety, to throw the light of Truth on its hidden ways of accomplishing evil, and to prove its powerlessness. She has given her followers the priceless knowledge of how to handle the claims of animal

63

magnetism, which oppose Christ's healing power. Each wise student of Christian Science gives careful heed and willing obedience to these instructions. She saw incredulity, hatred of the Truth, misrepresentation of herself and her motives fall into meaningless dust before the released power of Mind lived and demonstrated as the animating purpose of her life. She was neither dazed nor dazzled by the human scenes confronting her, and she was unmoved by the efforts of evil to exploit her personality. Principle, not person, was the basis of her healing work, and of the Church she founded.

Mrs. Eddy discovered and explored the power of Mind to heal and to remove the mists which would hide reality. She has made understandable the scientific fact that because man is never sick, mankind can be healed of their diseases. It is such knowing and proving that makes Christian Science as valuable in the age of space as when Jesus healed multitudes on the shores of Galilee. The love of Mrs. Eddy reached over zones and hemispheres, latitudes and longitudes, to bless. Her tireless labors for mankind evidence the energies of ministering Love. More than half a century ago when most men's horizons extended not much farther than their city or their nation, the universal love of this great woman inspired her to write, "From the interior of Africa to the utmost parts of the earth, the sick and the heavenly homesick or hungry hearts are calling on me for help, and I am helping them." [8]

The brotherhood of man is a divine reality, but the brotherhood of man without the fatherhood of God is a hollow dream, a human mockery of a spiritual fact. To reveal what God is and what the true nature of man is as His son—this was the inspiration of our Leader's healing works. These works go on. Each individual healed by reading her textbook, each life uplifted by a Christian Science church service, each seeker having the torch of his understanding lighted by her example of humility and devotion—these are the healing works of Mary Baker Eddy.

Practitioner

In selfless love she has followed the command of Christ Jesus, "Heal the sick, cleanse the lepers, raise the dead, cast out devils: freely ye have received, freely give." [9]

Behold how freely she has given!

[1] Retrospection and Introspection, p. 31
[2] Science and Health, p. 177
[3] John 5:19
[4] Science and Health, pp. 476, 477
[5] Acts 4:20
[6] Unity of Good by Mary Baker Eddy, p. 7
[7] Luke 11:20
[8] The First Church of Christ, Scientist, and Miscellany, p. 147
[9] Matthew 10:8

8

Mary Baker Eddy

Teacher and educator

by DeWitt John

After her great discovery of Christian Science, Mrs. Eddy faced an unparalleled challenge: to find ways of sharing her revelation with others.

Mighty was this challenge. It demanded awakening people to the opposite of their deepest convictions—to the allness of Spirit and the nothingness of matter. It called for showing them a totally new way of thinking: how to reason from a purely spiritual basis; how to practice the rules for metaphysical healing; how to proceed with deep, systematic, scientific prayer and treatment. It required steps to guard and transmit the pure teachings through the defiling centuries.

Among these steps was the founding of the educational system of Christian Science. Through an understanding of this educational system, Mrs. Eddy's magnificent achievements as a teacher and educator can best be appreciated.

From 1867 to 1898 Mrs. Eddy taught many students. In the process she perfected her methods and developed the text for classroom use we know as the chapter "Recapitulation" in "Science and Health with Key to the Scriptures." Today her educational system continues to carry on her work, bringing spiritual enlightenment and liberation to thousands.

Mary Baker Eddy:

What constitutes this system? Outwardly it includes provisions in the Manual of The Mother Church by Mrs. Eddy for preparation of teachers of Christian Science, for primary classes, and for annual association meetings of pupils. It includes the Sunday School. Also, Mrs. Eddy provided the means for orderly self-instruction in Christian Science. These include the Lesson-Sermons, outlined in the *Christian Science Quarterly,* which, with their twenty-six subjects, deal thoroughly and systematically with the basic teachings of Christian Science. Christian Scientists have also as invaluable auxiliaries to individual study and practice the Concordances to Mrs. Eddy's writings, initiated under her direction, and the standard Concordances to the Bible.

These are outward components. But the value of this educational system is to be found in its inner character.

Mrs. Eddy showed a consistently high regard for education and culture. But her system transcends commonly accepted teaching and learning processes. Yet her methods do not lower the worth of human concepts of education; rather do they uplift and enrich them.

Mrs. Eddy speaks of Christian Science as leading the ages. [1] This applies to its educational system. The system is revolutionary. It offers radical new insights into the art of enlightenment and effective communication.

This educational system does not rely on processes of the human mind but on revelation from the divine Mind. It does not include speculation from the standpoint of mortal ignorance but inspiration from the standpoint of Mind's omniscience. Its method of learning is not the accretion of finite human knowledge from without, but an unfolding of infinite divine consciousness, the kingdom of heaven, within.

One finds it illuminating to examine closely certain of the leading elements of Science. He will learn something of its scope and

Teacher and educator

depth, its practicality and revolutionary power. He will recognize also the remarkable consistency between Mrs. Eddy's own example as teacher and the requirements she has set for the educational system she established. What she herself demonstrated in teaching, she has enshrined in the standard provided for others.

Two main sources bear witness to these statements. One is the authorized reminiscences and biographies which tell of Mrs. Eddy's own classroom work. The other is her own writings, with their specific instructions and abundant guidance for both teaching and learning.

From these sources one gains a new sense of the magnitude of Mrs. Eddy's work as teacher and educator. The wholeness, coherence, and beauty of her educational system emerge in luminous grandeur and detail. One feels the God-impelled inspiration which animated her own teaching and which continues to invigorate the teaching work today.

Consider, for example, a leading element of this educational system: its purpose. Clearly the purpose is to prepare the student to practice Christian Science in healing.

Mrs. Eddy stressed this purpose in the classroom. In the class of 1885 she concluded the third day by saying, "Now go home and take your first patient." [2] When a student in the class of 1883 said she did not know what she was to do with what she was learning, Mrs. Eddy responded, "You are going to heal with it." [3]

With logical consistency our Leader makes clear in the Manual and in her other writings that the purpose of class instruction today is to enable the learner to heal and uplift others. Also, it is worthy of note how frequently the Lesson-Sermons stress the point that what is learned must be made practical in healing and actual demonstration. And how significantly for the Sunday School does Mrs. Eddy write in Science and Health, "The entire education of children should be such as to form habits of obedience to

71

the moral and spiritual law, with which the child can meet and master the belief in so-called physical laws, a belief which breeds disease." [4]

The aim of this educational system is consistent throughout: to equip the learner to demonstrate the Truth-power in healing.

Consider also, as another leading element, the standpoint from which the teaching is to be done. Mrs. Eddy illustrated the right standpoint in her own teaching. One of her students recalls, "She effaced the sense of her personality so completely that she thought, spoke, and acted from the standpoint of her oneness with the Father." [5]

Others have noted that Mrs. Eddy seemed to be a transparency for Truth to shine through; that she appeared to be conscious at all times of a wisdom beyond her own; that she maintained a listening attitude to hear what God would give her to say. Her selflessness and humility turned the students away from personality to the divine Principle of being.

Mrs. Eddy has called upon her followers to maintain this same standpoint in carrying on her educational system. She writes, "That teacher does most for his students who divests himself most of pride and self, and by reason thereof is able to empty his students' minds of error, that they may be filled with Truth." [6]

Another outstanding element of this educational system is its teaching method. Nothing could be more illuminating of Mrs. Eddy's greatness as a teacher than the record of how she taught. She dealt directly with the thought of each student. She taught by means of searching questions and answers.

One of her students records: "Her method in teaching was first to question the pupils. Her clear insight could detect at once whether they answered by merely repeating the words or from an understanding heart. After listening to the answers, she unfolded spiritual truths according to the need." [7]

Teacher and educator

Another student has written that when the class of 1885 first assembled, Mrs. Eddy stood before her pupils and looked quietly and searchingly at each one, taking direct mental cognizance of each; only after that did she speak. The biographer Lyman P. Powell observes that Mrs. Eddy understood the character and mental makeup of each one who attended her classes and sought to meet the need of each.

There is nothing superficial about the educational method of Christian Science. It goes far deeper than the activity of human intellect. The inspired teachings reach to the very foundations of one's consciousness. They awaken and purify. They work a transformation in one's whole being, filling consciousness with light.

Many of those who knew Mrs. Eddy have stressed her use of the question and answer method. She herself has specified that this same method is to be used in the teaching today. She writes, "Christian Scientists should take their textbook into the schoolroom the same as other teachers; they should ask questions from it, and be answered according to it,—occasionally reading aloud from the book to corroborate what they teach." [8] She has also provided in the Manual that the question and answer method shall be used in the Sunday School.

Mrs. Eddy makes clear that Christian Science cannot be thoroughly taught to large audiences, because the teaching requires addressing the pupils individually and examining critically the thoughts expressed. Clearly Mrs. Eddy felt that the teacher must deal with the thinking of each pupil. This calls for a thorough dissection of thoughts, a process which is necessary if the teacher is "to empty his students' minds of error, that they may be filled with Truth."

Another important element is the substance of what is taught. While the letter is important, the spirit is paramount. Much more is imparted than words alone. It is the Christ-spirit that makes

73

the teaching effective. Only those imbued with the spirit of genuine Christianity can teach Christian Science effectively. Only those imbued with the spirit of genuine Christianity can learn it effectively.

Mrs. Eddy's students uniformly record that she permitted no note-taking. One of them writes: "Her impartations transcended the medium of words. Words served only to convey her revelations. She gave both the letter and the spirit, but she took away the letter lest any should substitute it for the wine of the Spirit." [9]

Throughout the chapter in Science and Health entitled "Teaching Christian Science"—and, indeed, throughout her writings—Mrs. Eddy stresses the importance of imbibing the spirit of Christ, and demonstrating it daily, if one would really understand Christian Science. Repeatedly she stresses the truth voiced by Christ Jesus, "It is the spirit that quickeneth." [10]

Still another vital element of this educational system is the standard of scientific exactness to be observed.

Mrs. Eddy carefully specified this standard: the teaching must be systematic, thorough, characterized by law and order, purely spiritual and not merely mental; and however little might be taught or learned, it must be correct.

Mrs. Eddy's students have recorded that she was quick to detect any deviation by students from clear, correct Science and to point out the discrepancy. And she established careful safeguards to protect her educational system against adulteration or quackery. The Manual provides that students shall not be guided by their teacher's personal views, but by the Bible and Science and Health. It specifies that members of The Mother Church shall not use written formulas in treatment; that they shall not learn hypnotism or read spurious literature; and that teachers shall counsel their pupils habitually to study the Bible and Science and Health.

Divine Science is exact because it is the emanation of perfect Mind. In expressing it, the letter as well as the spirit must be right.

Teacher and educator

Science and Health stresses the necessity, in demonstrating Truth, of never deviating from pure and genuine Science, "Strict adherence to the divine Principle and rules of the scientific method has secured the only success of the students of Christian Science." [11] And Mrs. Eddy has provided that the same standard shall apply to the Sunday School, "The instruction given by the children's teachers must not deviate from the absolute Christian Science contained in their textbook." [12]

Much more could be said of other aspects of Mrs. Eddy's teaching and of her educational system. We could speak of the central place of the Scriptures in her teaching and her wonderful illumination of their spiritual meaning; of the vitally important requirement that teachers shall open the eyes of their pupils to the ways and deceptiveness of evil and its nothingness, thus equipping them to handle it and to protect themselves on the basis of evil's unreality and Truth's allness; of the moral and spiritual demands made on the teachers; of the requirements that pupils be morally sound, receptive, and ready for deep systematic thinking; and of the admonition that teachers are obligated, after the class term, to promote the continuing spiritual progress of their pupils but not to take personal control of them.

From start to finish the stress is on practice and proof in healing. What greater joy than to partake of such education!

It is revealing to make a list, from the sources mentioned above, of the moral and spiritual qualities expressed in Mrs. Eddy's own teaching. Her students have spoken of the courtesy, gentleness, tenderness, and love she expressed; of the youthfulness, wit, joy, radiancy, and beauty; of the discernment, incisiveness, lucidity, and brevity of statement; of the simplicity, humility, meekness; of her grasp, comprehensiveness, and depth; of the demonstrated spiritual power which so often had brought instantaneous cure; of her constant consciousness of divine Love's nearness and goodness and all-power; of her self-effacement and constant turning of the students' thoughts to the wondrous glories and immediate practicality of divine Love.

One recognizes here the redeeming power and presence of the immortal Christ. Here is the essence of effective teaching. It is the Christ that enlightens mankind, uplifts, heals, saves. The spirit of Christ reveals to the receptive thought man's absolute oneness with his Father-Mother God. When both teacher and student are imbued with the true spirit of Christ, the Scriptural prophecy is fulfilled, "They shall be all taught of God." [13]

Mrs. Eddy stressed this in her own teaching. And she has emphasized it in the loving provision she has made for the continuing work of her educational system, for example, "Of this also rest assured, that books and teaching are but a ladder let down from the heaven of Truth and Love, upon which angelic thoughts ascend and descend, bearing on their pinions of light the Christ-spirit." [14]

[1] Message to The Mother Church for 1901 by Mary Baker Eddy, p. 21
[2] We Knew Mary Baker Eddy, Second Series, p. 9
[3] Historical Sketches, p. 136
[4] Science and Health, p. 62
[5] We Knew Mary Baker Eddy, Second Series, p. 11
[6] Retrospection and Introspection, p. 84
[7] We Knew Mary Baker Eddy, First Series, p. 82
[8] Retrospection and Introspection, p. 83
[9] We Knew Mary Baker Eddy, Second Series, p. 8
[10] John 6:63
[11] Science and Health, p. 456
[12] Manual, Art. XX, Sect. 3
[13] John 6:45
[14] Retrospection and Introspection, p. 85

9

Her influence upon science

by F. Karl Willenbrock

The Discoverer and Founder of Christian Science, Mary Baker Eddy, spoke directly and forcefully about the natural sciences. The significance of her discovery is yet to be recognized in these fields of human study and research, but even now there are many evidences of the accuracy of her predictions about the growth of these sciences. The perspicacity of her analyses of their limitations has also become increasingly evident as their methodology has developed and has become better understood. While some of the implications of the teachings of Christian Science have already found their way into the development of the natural sciences, it appears probable that future developments will feel their impact even more.

The truth which Christian Science has presented to the world is in the process of leavening the thought of mortals. While the natural sciences are among the most prestigious and humanly successful modes of thought, they too are being influenced by the facts which have been brought to light by Mrs. Eddy. In the one hundred years since the discovery of Christian Science, tremendous changes have occurred in the natural sciences. They have grown from a small activity which concerned few individuals and had little effect on human society to a position of major importance in human affairs.

79

In her selection of the word "Science" to label her discovery, Mrs. Eddy was clearly raising the term to a new range of significance. She drew a sharp distinction between the Science of Christianity and what she termed "the ordinary scientific schools" when in "Science and Health with Key to the Scriptures" she wrote, "Because the Science of Mind seems to bring into dishonor the ordinary scientific schools, which wrestle with material observations alone, this Science has met with opposition." [1] Yet some characteristics of the natural sciences, such as the importance of accumulated evidence or demonstration rather than opinion, the utilization of logically consistent reasoning, and the need for understanding rather than simply belief, correspond to those of Christian Science. The designation of the term "Science" might well imply that the natural sciences as a branch of human knowledge have a significant role in the improvement of human existence.

Mrs. Eddy leaves no doubt that the natural sciences will not lead to an understanding of the facts of being. She indicates unequivocally that these sciences are based on the testimony of the physical senses which changes as new experimental observations are made. In contrast, Jesus of Nazareth did not use physical sense testimony as a guide to truth but rather turned to his Father, God. In answer to questioning, he asserted, "I receive not testimony from man." [2] In the same chapter, he also stated, "The Son can do nothing of himself, but what he seeth the Father do." [3] Thus he based his thought and actions on God, whom Mrs. Eddy has defined as Principle, a term which indicates His fixed and permanent nature. However, she also says: "Human thoughts have their degrees of comparison. Some thoughts are better than others." [4] Many of the thoughts which have characterized the developments of the natural sciences fit into this latter category of being better than their predecessors. To the extent that these thoughts have led to useful developments, which have helped to free men from the limitations imposed by the human mind, they are representative of the benefits which the increase of knowledge and the removal of ignorance can bring to human experience.

Perhaps an examination of some of the specific ways in which the natural sciences have progressed in the last century will illustrate this point. It is clear that this period has been one of great achievement, during which the natural sciences have given men increased freedom from physical limitations. These advances have extended men's physical capabilities in a number of ways: the development of microscopes, both light and electron, has extended men's capabilities to observe the very small; the development of telescopes, both light and radio, has enabled men to see farther into physical space than previously; the development of new propulsion systems has increased men's ability to travel at high speeds over great distances; the ability to control electromagnetic phenomena has increased men's ability to communicate over all parts of the globe; the development of automatic computing machines has enabled men to process numeric and non-numeric data at tremendously increased rates of speed. This progress has resulted from the ability to replace with better thoughts some of the ignorance which has limited mankind's capabilities for so long.

Mrs. Eddy describes this process where she writes: "If the eyes see no sun for a week, we still believe that there is solar light and heat. Science (in this instance named natural) raises the human thought above the cruder theories of the human mind, and casts out a fear." [5] This period of human history has been characterized by the casting aside of many of the cruder theories of the natural sciences, such as the concept of the universe as a huge mechanism controlled by mechanical forces and the concept of matter as composed of hard particles. In both of these cases, increasingly abstract views were needed to describe physical phenomena more accurately and to eliminate improper conclusions.

With these clearer views has come an increased ability to use these phenomena in the service of mankind. The resultant material benefits are indicative of the spiritual benefits to be gained from an increase in spiritual understanding, which will not simply satisfy some human needs but will provide for all of mankind's needs.

Mrs. Eddy's examination of the methodology of the natural sciences has exposed their limitations. Since they are dependent on physical sense testimony, they clearly cannot lead to an understanding of the spiritual universe or spiritual man. In their preoccupation with matter's organization, characteristics, and behavior, natural scientists are not approaching the spiritualization of thought which will lead them to the spiritual facts or even to the recognition of the true nature of matter and the physical universe. Mrs. Eddy warns, "Matter cannot connect mortals with the true origin and facts of being, in which all must end." [6] In this way she has described the outer limit to which the natural sciences can aspire; that is, they can develop useful inventions but will not lead to the ultimate facts which underlie true being.

Although it is not evident that many natural scientists have seen the limitations of their sciences with such clarity, it is undoubtedly true that fewer and fewer now feel that their methods are applicable to all fields of human learning. It has become clear that an essential characteristic of the natural sciences is their utilization of quantitative measurement and mathematical deduction. Ethical and aesthetic values, for example, are not susceptible to such detailed quantitative measure and so lie outside the realm of the natural sciences.

In her analysis of the ultimate nature of matter and the physical universe, Mrs. Eddy goes far beyond the present understanding of the natural scientist. Her statement, "The physical universe expresses the conscious and unconscious thoughts of mortals," [7] is not approached in current theories of physics or astronomy.

Her influence upon science

However, this statement does throw light on some of the speculations of prominent natural scientists. Albert Einstein, in his essay "Physics and Reality," writes, "The eternal mystery of the world is its comprehensibility." To the natural scientist, it is not clear that there is any relation between the human mind and the physical universe. If none is assumed to exist, there is no *a priori* reason for believing that the physical universe is comprehensible to the human mind. But Mrs. Eddy's explanation that this universe expresses mortal thinking leads directly to the reason why it is comprehensible to human thought and to an explanation of Einstein's "eternal mystery."

In another thought-provoking statement, Mrs. Eddy writes with reference to physical science, "When this human belief lacks organizations to support it, its foundations are gone." [8] To most natural scientists, natural science is a description of external objects which have an objective status independent of human observers or of any other form of subjective support. Therefore it is of interest to note that Mrs. Eddy's statement is approached by a highly respected physicist and philosopher of science, Henry Margenau, of Yale University, who has written concerning physical facts, "Actually, they are supported in a fluid medium called theory, or theoretical interpretation, a medium which prevents them from collapsing into insignificance."

To the extent that these statements are indicative of advanced thinking in the natural sciences, they show there is much yet to be learned by leading thinkers before reaching the conclusions about the natural sciences that Mrs. Eddy perceived through her understanding of the Science of being. But the fact should not be overlooked that these statements which define the essence of the physical universe and physical science have entered mortal thought and started the leavening process. The lack of present acceptance in no way detracts from their significance or importance. Their full impact on mortal thought is yet to be felt.

A most significant contribution to the future development of the natural sciences has been made by Mrs. Eddy in helping to free mankind from the self-imposed limitation which comes from the acceptance of the human mind as the source of intelligence and as the instrument upon which future progress is dependent. The freedom which Christian Science brings from such misconceptions should enable those with spiritual understanding to extend their capabilities beyond what is presently being demonstrated. As the understanding of Christian Science expands in human thinking, its influence can be only in the direction of improving the ability of all men to demonstrate increasingly their potentialities for improved clarity of thought and capacity for learning. The natural sciences have developed historically by the contributions of a relatively small number of great men. The effect of Christian Science should be to increase the number and capabilities of such individuals.

As mankind's thinking becomes more and more imbued with spiritual sense, which is man's capacity to discern enduring verities, the facts concerning the spiritual universe will become better understood. The order which characterizes it will become increasingly apparent to human thought, and inharmonies of human thought will be lessened or supplanted. As human thought develops in this way into a more ordered state, the physical universe which expresses it should also show an increase in order and thus become more comprehensible to the natural scientist who studies it.

In the chapter entitled "Genesis" in Science and Health, Mrs. Eddy analyzes from a metaphysical standpoint some of the theories of the natural sciences prevalent at that time. She illustrates how it is possible with the aid of Christian Science to distinguish among the various assumptions made by natural scientists in their attempts to understand physical phenomena and to select the least erroneous ones. In effect, she utilizes the spiritual facts of being

Her influence upon science

to eliminate the more unsound theories and to seek those theories which are more in accord with the Science of being.

In a similar fashion, the metaphysician of today should develop the capability of bringing to bear on the current theories of the natural sciences the insight which is characteristic of spiritual sense. With this insight, he should help to guide those theories in the direction of increasing validity and usefulness in the human realm. As her followers develop the spiritual stature needed, they will increase Mrs. Eddy's influence on the natural sciences for the benefit of all mankind.

[1] Science and Health, p. 483
[2] John 5:34;   [3] 5:19
[4] Science and Health, p. 297;   [5] p. 189;   [6] p. 491;   [7] p. 484;   [8] p. 124

10

Her influence upon theology

by Allison W. Phinney, Jr.

Many years ago a meteor fell into the forests of Siberia, but not until much later, when the region had been completely explored, was the vastness of the impact understood. In a sense, the impact of Christian Science on theology has been made, but its significance has not yet been widely explored or acknowledged.

In the Preface of "Science and Health with Key to the Scriptures," Mary Baker Eddy, the Discoverer and Founder of Christian Science, writes, "A book introduces new thoughts, but it cannot make them speedily understood." She adds, "Future ages must declare what the pioneer has accomplished." [1]

It is plain from Mrs. Eddy's exchanges with clergymen of her day and from her many references to theology that she knew the magnitude of the challenge Christian Science presents to the mode of thought she sometimes called "scholastic" or "speculative theology." Inspired theology, on the other hand—the clear, healing reasoning on God's allness which flows forth from having that "mind . . . which was also in Christ Jesus" [2]—she recognized as the keystone of the Science of Christianity.

The subject of theology is by definition God. But the theologian has no special access to divinity. Only radical yielding to God can illumine thought and bring forth rightness and healing in human experience. This is as true for the individual who is a professional theologian as for the housewife, the engineer, or the businessman.

89

For centuries Christian theologies have reasoned academically about God. In effect they have dealt with Him as one aspect of a material cosmos which proceeds otherwise along the lines the material senses suggest. God has been taken as a logical starting point for creation. His influence has been seen primarily in long-range terms. He has been held to be setting His creation gradually right after mankind chose sin and fell from paradise.

God has been considered to be transcendent, unknowable, except in rare mystic experiences. To most Christians, He has been known primarily through a supernatural event in the past, when He supposedly took on flesh in the form of Christ Jesus, sacrificed the Son to cancel the debt of sin, and restored the possibility of salvation to those who would faithfully confess the fact of this event.

One can see that this is a thin outline which those might construct who felt remote from the immense, convincing truths and healing experiences of the Word made flesh. It persists in varying forms today because it is the outcome of thought which begins with matter as the most basic aspect of reality and then reasons toward God.

Mrs. Eddy explains that prior to her discovery of Christian Science the illusion of security in material birth, life, and death had been shattered. In the experience which led directly to her discovery, she turned wholly to God. She writes, "That short experience included a glimpse of the great fact that I have since tried to make plain to others, namely, Life in and of Spirit; this Life being the sole reality of existence." [3] The divine was no longer felt to be waiting above and at the end of human history. It was seen as Immanuel, or "God with us," breaking forth into human experience inevitably in transformation and healing!

In selfless, fearless moments great religious figures had caught sight of the Principle, or Love, at the heart of being. But evil had claimed overpowering immediacy, and the sense of God's presence

Her influence upon theology

had seemed to slip away. Through revelation, reason, and demonstration, Mrs. Eddy learned that evil is never real. She saw objectively (as much so as in a natural scientist's study of molecular behavior) that evil exists entirely within mesmerized, fearing, unperceiving thought, or that which St. Paul termed the carnal mind, which is "enmity against God." [4] To the question "What is the cardinal point of the difference in my metaphysical system?" Mrs. Eddy replies, "This: that *by knowing the unreality of disease, sin, and death,* you demonstrate the allness of God." [5]

The influence of Christian Science was felt first by the pure of heart, who responded openly to the spirit of the Christ and for whom dogma and ecclesiasticism were not authoritative.

As one sits quietly in the original edifice of The Mother Church today and sees as through the eyes of those who first attended services the inscriptions on the walls from the Bible and Mrs. Eddy's writings, one can easily experience again the impact of the coming of Christian Science. The healing touch of the Christ was being felt as in the time of the Master. This was no weighing of theological pros and cons but the direct experience of a totally new reality which once seen would not permit one to see the world in the same way as before. It was not mystical, theoretical, nor emotional. As today, it was the breaking of fear and limitations, the bearing onward of spiritual insight, the fading of the dissonance and chaos of material living as unnatural, unreal.

Mrs. Eddy writes, "Jesus established in the Christian era the precedent for all Christianity, theology, and healing." [6] The Gospel of John tells of the meeting of the disciples with a man who had been born blind. They fell into discussion of a theological question, attributing the man's blindness to sin. The question of whether the man or his parents had sinned was taken to the Master. But Jesus, so filled with the compelling reality of man's unity with the Father, moved immediately to restore the man's sight. The irresistible truth of God's presence eliminated any dark supposition of His absence. The mistaken perspective in which the disciples' question arose had ceased to exist.

The coming of Christian Science placed old theological arguments in a clear, intense light. Throughout history theologians as well as natural scientists had taken matter as self-evident. Mrs. Eddy drew the issue with the point of a sword. She writes thus of the dilemma of matter: "To seize the first horn of this dilemma and consider matter as a power in and of itself, is to leave the creator out of His own universe; while to grasp the other horn of the dilemma and regard God as the creator of matter, is not only to make Him responsible for all disasters, physical and moral, but to announce Him as their source, thereby making Him guilty of maintaining perpetual misrule in the form and under the name of natural law." [7]

Academic theologians and philosophers had considered this issue before. But in men's experience in the twentieth century it was to be sharpened to a cutting edge.

From the time of the Renaissance, academic theology was progressively forced to give up its comfortable province of discussing a supernatural and highly imaginary cosmogony. Then in the mid-nineteenth century the pressure of natural science suddenly increased. Work in the fields of anthropology, psychology, astronomy, physics, and genetics steadily pushed back the claims of religion to describe the workings of even the visible material world as God-directed. With the twentieth century came more universal concepts of love and justice, together with such an overwhelming knowledge of the extent of mankind's suffering that few could link it any longer with a coherent divine plan.

Religious thinking was heavily influenced by the apparent darkness of the human situation. Existential philosophy probed the anxiety and absurdity of mortal life. The dominant theology of

these years, known as neoorthodoxy or "crisis" theology, emphasized men's hopelessly sinful plight. Man, it is said, could only
throw himself on the mercy of the distant historical event of God's
coming to earth in Christ Jesus.

Other theologians currently stress the suffering of Jesus and his
love for others, suggesting that it is God's purpose to make man
live a supremely unselfed life in the world without resting on any
hope of intervention by God. The "absence of God" or the "death
of God" so far as modern men are concerned is widely discussed.
Long-established concepts of a supernatural God have been shaken
for many religious thinkers.

Mrs. Eddy writes, "As the finite sense of Deity, based on material conceptions of spiritual being, yields its grosser elements, we
shall learn what God is, and what God does." [8] At present the
spiritually awakening thought of humanity wrestles desperately
with the supposition of a tragically imperfect material universe in
which there seems so little evidence of an infinitely good and
omnipotent God. But great changes in theology in only a century's
time foreshadow the outcome of this long conflict.

Today increasing numbers of religious men readily conceive of
God as Love and are reluctant to attribute anthropomorphic atti-
tudes to Him. The concept of the atonement has moved from that
of satisfying a wrathful God's justice toward that of reconciling
man to God, to his true relationship with the Father. Heaven and
hell are now widely understood as states of thought, not as distant
localities in which reward and punishment are to be administered.
Prayer is more frequently recognized as the awakening of men to
God's healing ever-presence, rather than as obtaining His change
of heart toward a human situation.

There is greater readiness to accept the possibility and the
necessity of apprehending the meaning of Jesus' teachings through
the illumination of the Christ in one's own life. Profession of a

93

creed is seen as a less and less adequate expression of Christianity. There are constant demands for demonstration of the spirit of the Christ in some way in the midst of the human experience.

Perhaps most significant is the breakdown of the ancient artificial line between the so-called sacred and the secular. Two of the theologians in modern times who have received the greatest response to their writings—Paul Tillich and Martin Buber—have stressed the divine as a dimension of reality which is always present in every human activity and in which "all things are become new." [9] To a limited extent, they have turned from the external world and a supernatural imposition upon it and looked within to their own deepest intuition of Love and of Spirit.

As Mrs. Eddy discerned would be the case in the twentieth century, Christian Science has led to the recovery of healing through spiritual means in the Christian churches. Calvinism had considered the New Testament healings the evidence of "miraculous powers" of "temporary duration." Clergymen turning anew to the Gospel accounts are becoming convinced of something far different.

One recent denominational report on "The Relation of Christian Faith to Health" observes: "He [Jesus] regarded the healings which took place as so many signs of God's power breaking in upon the kingdom of evil. . . . He [Jesus Christ] regarded illness as something to be overcome. He did not acquiesce to it. He did not ignore it. . . . He coped with illness, and he conquered it. It was his teaching that God wills healing." Similar reports specifically mention the part Christian Science has played in a reawakening to the "New Testament teaching about God's will for us to be healed and to be whole."

Healing services are carried on regularly in hundreds of Episcopal and Methodist churches in the United States. Other denominations have established commissions to investigate the possibility of spiritual healing. Extreme differences remain between the theology

Her influence upon theology

and practice of Christian Science and that of other denominations. But for any awareness of the healing presence of "God with us," Christian Scientists feel the most earnest gratitude.

Mrs. Eddy points out, "The confidence inspired by Science lies in the fact that Truth is real and error is unreal." [10] The impact of the Science of Christianity will be continuously explored in our time and in centuries to come. The lesson of its unequivocal statement of the allness of God, Spirit, the nothingness of matter, and the perfect or new man as the present scientific fact will be learned. The deep Christianity of its insight into the hypnotic, illusory nature of evil will be gained. The joy and good which men have thought fragile and fleeting will be found again and again the essence, the structure, the entire substance of real being.

[1] Science and Health, p. vii
[2] Philippians 2:5
[3] Miscellaneous Writings, p. 24
[4] Romans 8:7
[5] Unity of Good, pp. 9, 10
[6] Science and Health, p. 138;   [7] p. 119
[8] The People's Idea of God, p. 2
[9] II Corinthians 5:17
[10] Science and Health, p. 368

11

Mary Baker Eddy

Her influence upon medicine

by John M. Tutt

A centenary is a period of one hundred years. It is also an evaluation of such a period. When Mary Baker Eddy discovered Christian Science in 1866 and later gave her discovery to the world in the Christian Science textbook, "Science and Health with Key to the Scriptures," she cut sharply across many accepted standards of thought and conduct and challenged us to higher issues. Her discovery that all is divine Mind and its manifestation as idea had a shocking impact upon the materially-minded; yet to the open-minded it came as release from the choking cords of matter limitation.

Christian Science teaches that all reality is a continuity. Creation itself is a continuing unfolding of God's thought. By its infinite nature God's thought, though complete, is never ended. Christian Science therefore is more than mere impact upon human consciousness and life. It is influence. It is a sustained inflowing of power to effect change for the better, to reverse false laws of matter and uphold true laws of Spirit.

There was a strong element of prophecy in Christ Jesus' parable of the kingdom of heaven likened to "leaven, which a woman took, and hid in three measures of meal, till the whole was leavened." [1] Our Leader declares: "In all mortal forms of thought, dust is dignified as the natural status of men and things, and modes of material motion are honored with the name of *laws*. This continues until the leaven of Spirit changes the whole of mortal thought, as yeast changes the chemical properties of meal." [2]

The leaven of Spirit is the influence Mrs. Eddy hid in the measure of meal called material medicine. Christian Science is mentalizing the whole world of matter; and chemicalization, or change from the materially mental to the divinely mental, is bringing forth a new conception of the healing art. This new creature conforms to the teaching and healing of Christ Jesus and is purely spiritual, not material. This is the effect of Christian Science as stated thus: "Through Christian Science, religion and medicine are inspired with a diviner nature and essence; fresh pinions are given to faith and understanding, and thoughts acquaint themselves intelligently with God." [3]

Mrs. Eddy grew up in an atmosphere of orthodox religion and medicine. Her spiritual-mindedness caused her, even as a child, to dissent from some of the teachings of the Congregational church, which she attended. A frail physicality incited her search for relief from bodily ills in various systems of healing. She studied homeopathy and became adept in its practice. All material methods failing her, she turned to God. This was natural to her, for she from childhood had been God-conscious and a devoted Bible student. In the teachings and practice of Jesus, Mrs. Eddy found the central oneness of true religion and medicine. Mrs. Eddy's own healing through her unquestioning faith in God's power and promise to heal was like the falling apple, which led her to the discovery of the Science of Christ and the applicability of divine law to the cure of the ills of humanity.

In healing the sick and sinning through purely spiritual means and methods, Christ Jesus disclaimed that he had come to destroy the law or the prophets and affirmed his mission to be one of fulfillment. Christian Science is leavening the human beliefs of healing

Her influence upon medicine

and saving, changing them from matter to Spirit, to the fulfillment of the mission of Christ Jesus.

In the Christian Science textbook, Materia Medica is recommended to adopt Christian Science (see p. 441). The influence of Christian Science on medicine is to free it from the limitations of its matter basis and to elevate the healing art to an all-powerful spiritual status. This is far from destructive but is evolutionary; indeed, it is revolutionary. It maintains the fundamental truth that the truly important understanding of anything is the spiritual; and that all genuine progress is the resolution of the material, or finite, and the attainment of spiritual reality. As regards material medicine, this cannot mean the absorption of Christian Science into material medicine. It means the adoption of Spirit, whereby medicine can cry, "Abba, Father." [4] The leaven of Spirit is at work in this mode of mortal thought as in all others and must continue till the entire material structure is replaced by the new creature.

Let us examine the structure of the lower concepts of medicine as Mrs. Eddy found it a hundred years ago. In essence it did not differ from the material medicine of Christ Jesus' day. It built upon matter and the material so-called mind. Indeed, the history of material medicine is contemporary with the human race and essentially unchanged. Over the millennia there have been ceaseless refinements, and these alterations have been called advancement in medicine.

It is interesting that the Greek word for "medicine" *(pharmakon),* from which is derived the word "pharmacy," has a spread of meaning from witchcraft, sorcery, magic, philters, to poisons, drugs, etc. Thus we see that material medicine has always been built upon matter and the material so-called mind. God, Spirit, the divine Mind, is not in all its ways. Yet its basic intent and endeavor are to relieve distress and to cure the ills of the human race. Unhappily so humane and altruistic a purpose can rise no higher than the chains which shackle it to matter will allow. Indeed, the mind of

101

matter can never be other than materially mental. Psychology as it is taught in the schools proposes a mind produced by physical reaction in the brain. So this so-called science of the mind waits on the physical laboratory of the brain.

Christian Science is leavening the mass of material medicine, however slowly. The influence of Christian Science upon medicine is toward the elimination of matter and the mind of matter from both theory and practice. It is easy to see in terms of time how it is that the adoption of Christian Science by material medicine has been and may be a gradual development. Consider that the five physical senses unite in testimony to the actuality of matter. They bear witness that matter is, that it is creative, that it is destructive, that it is curative. Only Christian Science can resolve the contradictions in those pronouncements of the senses. Only through the higher senses of the divine Mind, God, can people be convinced that what causes disease cannot be relied upon to cure it. And yet already the need for recognition of the mental cause of disease has developed the neurology of the material medicine of Mrs. Eddy's time into the psychiatry of today. And while psychiatry does not rise above material medicine, it has served to refine it further toward the Christianly scientific resolution of material things into their falsely mental gist; and that step is preparatory to the final step of replacement of such false conceptions with right ideas. Christian Science alone can supply these correct ideas of man's true status of perfection as the creation of divine Mind, God.

Christian Science offers material medicine the same scheme of salvation from disease and sin that Christ Jesus came to preach, to teach, and to demonstrate. The way to health and to holiness is the same. John the Baptist came preaching it, "Repent ye: for the kingdom of heaven is at hand." [5] Christ Jesus came preaching and practicing it. Health and holiness are the same wholeness, the unity of Father and son, of God and man. The high idealism of the Hippocratic oath can never be realized without the renunciation of matter.

The writer took the Hippocratic oath and looked forward to its realization in medical practice. But he found himself tied to the theory that matter devours its own progeny and has all the mixture of vices and virtues of the Greek mythology. He was forced at last to accept the apostle's warning, "Doth a fountain send forth at the same place sweet water and bitter?" [6] Happily for him he found the answer in John's cry, "Repent ye." This change of mind from matter to Spirit is the ultimate of the leavening in individual thought and in material medicine. The Psalmist boldly declared, "I will walk in mine integrity." [7] And so the leaven of Truth a woman took and hid in the healing and saving modes of human thought will eventually entirely free religion and medicine from the disintegrating contamination of matter and the false mind that forms matter things and again unite them in the Science of the one Mind. There can be no doubt that Christ Jesus' religion and medicine were one and based on Spirit, not matter; on the divine Mind and not on a matter-based mind. His psychology was not a sound mind in a sound body but a sound body in a sound Mind, on earth even as it is in heaven.

What is medicine? This is a pertinent question in considering Mrs. Eddy's influence upon medicine. Everybody is born under the belief that matter is creative, and without Christian Science, brought up on the belief that matter is destructive and that matter is curative. The paradoxes involved in these beliefs present contrasts such as certain forms of matter endowed with curative qualities in minor quantities and poisonous power in larger dosage. Wholesomeness up to a point, disintegration from there on—an intermingling of good and evil, of truth and error.

Through the centuries matter curative agents have multiplied until their name is Legion. The present influx of synthetic chemical compounds under the terms antibiotics and sulfa drugs, commonly called wonder drugs, presents the familiar mixing of good and evil qualities to an extent that gravely concerns the medical faculty because of the appearance of new diseases under the administration of many of these new products. A new term has been necessary to describe these new diseases. They are called iatrogenic, and that means diseases caused by doctors. And the doctors rightly are concerned, and they are insisting on greater care in the use of such remedies. All of which calls for a more adequate definition of medicine. And this is obvious when we consider that there is scarcely a form of matter that has not been used as medicine. There is not an item of food in the kitchen, pantry, or on the dining table that probably is not or has not been a medicine in the apothecary shop. Even water can be so regarded, as well as climate, height, depth, sea, mountain, and desert.

The conclusion is inescapable that medicine is not matter. Medicine is comprised wholly in mental consent. The material mind which makes its thought objective in matter things determines also the so-called curative power. And the individual through his consent or dissent determines whether they are medicine to him. Whatever one believes is or may be curative or palliative is to him medicine. And his mental rejection of the medical laws of mortal mind nullifies them.

The writer has personal knowledge of an individual who was unaffected by lethal doses of morphine and strychnine. It has been demonstrated that hypodermic injections of distilled water have been a definite pain reliever. The Christian Scientist has but one medicine—the healing and saving power of Christ, the spiritual idea of God, the divine Mind. This "power of God unto salvation," [8] as Paul put it, this Christ, is defined in Science and Health thus: "CHRIST. The divine manifestation of God, which comes to the flesh to destroy incarnate error." [9]

Material medicine, then, is false belief in matter as curative. And a false belief never rises above the status of misunderstanding or misstatement. It can never be an actual state. Christ, the curative and preventive power of Truth, is not merely statement; it is state, condition, actuality. The Christ of God is the consciousness of the harmony of Soul to the preclusion of false beliefs about the body, about man; and this power over incarnate error of belief is operative on earth to cure and prevent, even as it is in heaven, to preserve the eternal wholeness of God and man.

The influence of Christian Science upon medicine can be only spiritual. Christ Jesus taught and practiced spiritually, which must be highest medicine. Mrs. Eddy brought to bear upon popular medicine the higher conceptions which Jesus knew and employed in healing the sick. Modern medicine cannot dismiss the Principle and the practice of the medicine of Christ Jesus. Without God, how can material medicine do the Christly healings?

Christ Jesus taught, preached, and healed. These three are one and inseparable. Yet we have the unnatural disunity of them, as witnessed in the diverse systems of secular teaching minus God, secular medicine without God, and preaching overloaded with doctrine and dogma. Mrs. Eddy found this triunity divorced and unrelated in home and school and church; and healing turned over to a system unmarked by spiritual content.

The influence of Mrs. Eddy upon medicine can be only divinely mental. Christian Science challenges all disease as mortally mental. It furnishes the answer to Macbeth's query, "Canst thou not minister to a mind diseas'd?" Mental sickness can be met only by divinely mental means. Matter-based mental methods directed against matter-based mental disease rise no higher than their source, brainology.

Christ Jesus challenged material medicine and popular and ecclesiastical orthodox standards. The response began unobtrusively in the individual human consciousness of the people in all classes—the fishermen, the publicans, the Roman and Jewish rulers, the poor, the rich, irrespective of persons. Christ Jesus furnished the proof of spiritual healing and left the spiritual leaven to spread. This is the picture today of the influence of Christian

Science upon the healing art. This is the working of the leaven a woman hid in medicine. It is changing the very nature and source of medicine and eventually will change the thought and attitude and practice of the popular and the professional mind.

Even though in the individual, God is not yet in all his ways, the leaven of Spirit will progressively bring God into his ways till finally God will indeed be in all his ways. The true idea of medicine will prevail, and the crossover from matter to mortal mind beliefs will find conclusion in the divinely mental and the full meaning and power of "Christ in you, the hope of glory" [10] and no less the surety of healing.

One of the qualities of Mary Baker Eddy's greatness was the patience with which she awaited the eventuality of her hopes and aims. She knew that God's time is not the interim between human events but is the unfolding of ideas. It was enough that the leaven of Spirit was planted in the human conception of medicine. Her prescience and her expectation were not pitched to the passing of years but to the leavening of the whole of medical thought and practice. One hundred years have passed, and we rightly note a centennial. But even as our great Leader knew, we too can understand with the Psalmist, "For a thousand years in thy sight are but as yesterday when it is past, and as a watch in the night." [11]

[1] Matthew 13:33
[2] Science and Health, p. 118;   [3] p. 107
[4] Romans 8:15
[5] Matthew 3:2
[6] James 3:11
[7] Psalm 26:11
[8] Romans 1:16
[9] Science and Health, p. 583
[10] Colossians 1:27
[11] Psalm 90:4

12

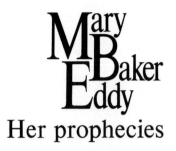

Her prophecies

by L. Ivimy Gwalter

Christian Science, its movement, and its Leader stride on. In "The First Church of Christ, Scientist, and Miscellany," Mrs. Eddy writes, "We thank the Giver of all good for the marvellous speed of the chariot-wheels of Truth and for the steadfast, calm coherence in the ranks of Christian Science." [1] No human pen or power fosters the spiritual impulsion of this forward march; no human pen or power can stop it. Its impetus is incorporeal, divine, as compelling as the coming of the daylight, yet as silent as the night.

Christian Science, its movement, and its Leader are divinely ordained, sustained, and protected. They sprang from Spirit and demonstrate the omnipotence, omnipresence, and omniscience of Spirit. Hence their vitality and permanence.

Prophecy as understood in Christian Science is the discernment of spiritual reality and its inevitable fulfillment in human experience. The thread of prophecy gleams in the first chapter of Genesis where it is affirmed that God created man in His own image, male and female, and commanded him to replenish and subdue the earth. It runs through the Old Testament. It shines resplendent in the earthly life of Christ Jesus, the masculine representative of Truth. It glows in the book of Revelation. And, as this series of articles has indicated, it comes to glorious fulfillment in the advent of Mary Baker Eddy, who, in her fulfillment of prophecy, typifies

109

the spiritual idea symbolized by the woman in the twelfth chapter of the Apocalypse.

But the thread of prophecy does not stop here. It reaches on and on as the mists of materialism dissolve and the great revelation gathers momentum and clearness. Through Mrs. Eddy, and through her alone, Christian Science has been presented to this age. She recognized this Science as the second coming of the Christ, the Comforter foretold by Jesus. She is the Discoverer and Founder of Christian Science and will forever remain its acknowledged Leader.

Mrs. Eddy's discovery was not the product of human reason but of divine revelation. She speaks of herself as a scribe whose orders came from heaven (see Miscellaneous Writings, p. 311). But she was more than a person transcribing a heavenly message. Her spiritual stature transcends mortal measurement. She is one with the revelation; through her the revelation speaks. The old adage, "What thou seest, that thou beest," is literally true of her.

Thus Mrs. Eddy's prophecies are not human prognostications. They are not the wishful thinking or chimerical fancy of a person. They grew out of her humility, the humility which enabled her to receive from God and give to the world the complete and final revelation of Truth. They are God's self-revealment of His own eternal power and glory subduing the earth—chastening and mellowing human thought in the coincidence of the human and the divine.

Mrs. Eddy's prophecies stem from the same source as the revelation. They are inspired utterances of present spiritual facts, reversing and refuting the evidence of the material senses. True prophecy illustrates the words of the Preacher: "I know that, whatsoever God doeth, it shall be for ever. . . . That which hath been is now; and that which is to be hath already been; and God requireth that which is past." [2] The prophecies of Mary Baker

Her prophecies

Eddy are impartations of divinity, pronouncements of divine purpose; hence their force and their inescapable fulfillment.

From the human standpoint prophecy implies futurity. In reality it indicates the yielding of material sense to the absoluteness of God, His ever-present supremacy and perfection. Prophecy holds within itself certainty and promise. Mrs. Eddy was as certain of ultimate harmony as she was of her own existence. She saw perfection not in the distant future but as present reality— tangible, knowable, provable. Page after page of her writings confirms this fact and agrees with the Master's statement, "Neither shall they say, Lo here! or, lo there! for, behold, the kingdom of God is within you." [3]

Mrs. Eddy's spiritual insight was her spiritual foresight. In "Science and Health with Key to the Scriptures," she writes, "It is the prerogative of the ever-present, divine Mind, and of thought which is in rapport with this Mind, to know the past, the present, and the future." [4] And then she explains divine Mind-reading as the opposite of clairvoyance and an essential element in Christianly scientific healing. Based on the Master's teachings, her prophecies are spiritual utterances of the certain operation of divine law in human affairs.

Her published writings are filled with prophecies which every student can find and record for himself. These prophecies coincide in all points with the inspired Word of the Bible. They foretell the solution of every human problem. It takes humility to understand these prophecies, and love and obedience to fathom the unerring divine Principle which underlies them.

Many of Mrs. Eddy's prophecies are already being fulfilled. Through divine revelation she discovered the absolute allness of God, Spirit, the unchanging spirituality of man and the universe, and the consequent nothingness of matter and evil. She foresaw the material resistance and growing mental opposition which this

111

revelation is today encountering. Indeed, she herself encountered this resistance and proved its powerlessness. In the course of her unique mission as Founder of Christian Science, evil rose often to engulf this great pioneer of Truth. But she rose still higher, founding her lifework ever more firmly on the rock of Christ.

She foresaw that, as this final revelation steadily presses its claims on mortals, human thought will undergo great changes. Divine Truth will transform the world; the universal language will be Christian healing, the new tongue of Spirit; and Christ, the true idea of God in divine Science, will finally govern all nations and peoples. Thus at last shall man in God's likeness, governed by Soul, not by corporeal sense, appear.

The revelation of God as divine Mind and of Spirit as All-in-all brought also the demonstration of the nothingness of matter. This truth is powerfully set forth in "the scientific statement of being," which begins, "There is no life, truth, intelligence, nor substance in matter." [5] By reducing all things material to their common denominator, mortal mind, Christian Science translates things into thoughts. Through its healing works Science proves unmistakably the illusive nature of this so-called mortal mind and its erroneous concepts. Through its demonstration of God as the only Mind, Science supplants material sense with spiritual sense and replaces the objects of mortal thought with spiritual ideas. Mrs. Eddy prophetically foresaw that this replacement will continue until all matter finally disappears in the crucible of Spirit.

Starting with the allness of Spirit and the nothingness of matter, the sovereignty of Love and the powerlessness of hate, Christian Science is today repeating, in the measure that it is understood, the works of the Master in the healing of sin, disease, and death.

Mrs. Eddy saw that the elements and functions of the human body will change as human thought becomes more spiritual and man's identity in God's likeness is understood; that health will be sought and found in Mind instead of in matter; and that, in

Her prophecies

fulfillment of Biblical prophecy, longevity will continue to increase until "death is swallowed up in victory." [6] Mrs. Eddy's prophecies include the final destruction of all sin, all disease, all death, as mortality yields to immortality, to the tender, resistless might of everlasting Life and Love.

Christian Science is potent to heal all manner of disease, but its primary mission is the destruction of sin and the evangelization of the human self. In her writings Mrs. Eddy foretells the world-wide moral upheaval and chemicalization that is now taking place. She sees this mental fermentation as a spiritual quickening which human thought is undergoing as Truth brings evil to the surface and destroys it.

She saw that in this chemicalization Christian Science and ani-mal magnetism—the term by which she designates all evil—will both be understood. She saw too that mankind, its eyes opened, will detect and chain the wickedness of the carnal mind by which it is being deceived. She writes, "The thunder of Sinai and the Sermon on the Mount are pursuing and will overtake the ages, rebuking in their course all error and proclaiming the kingdom of heaven on earth." [7] And she adds: "Truth is revealed. It needs only to be practised."

Her prophecies foretell the blessings that will flow from the spiritualization of human thought as Christian Science is more generally understood and demonstrated. Electricity in whatever form will be shown harmless. Changes in the physical universe will progressively dissolve material limitations. War will cease. Marriage will undergo purification, and divine Love will be found wedded to its own immaculate idea. Human law will become more penetrating and human justice more divine. Education will develop along spiritual lines. Christian healing by spiritual means alone will supersede material remedies and will be scientifically practiced by Christendom as a whole. The brotherhood of man will follow mankind's acceptance of the fatherhood and motherhood of God;

113

and all nations, peoples, and races will find their place and their inalienable rights in His kingdom.

Similarly Mrs. Eddy saw the dangers threatening governments and nations. She saw the encroachment of false systems of mental and physical control, of occultism, bigotry, and envy, of selfishness, apathy, and deceit. And she saw that mankind's progress Spiritward will at last break the fetters of evil and that this progress can never be hindered or reversed. In "No and Yes," she writes: "Progress, legitimate to the human race, pours the healing balm of Truth and Love into every wound. It reassures us that no Reign of Terror or rule of error will again unite Church and State, or reenact, through the civil arm of government, the horrors of religious persecution." [8]

Mrs. Eddy's faith in the ultimate triumph of the Science of Christianity, taught by Christ Jesus and brought to this age through her God-impelled discovery, could not be shaken. She saw that Christianity in its glorious Science is destined to become the one and only religion on this planet, and that the Church of Christ, Scientist, foreshadows the Church Universal and Triumphant. And she saw the permanence of The Mother Church and its branches, and the supreme authority of the divinely ordained Manual of The Mother Church, of which she is the author. Through the inspired textbook, Science and Health, she speaks as Pastor Emeritus at every service of the Church of Christ, Scientist, the world over. Thus with uncompromising courage she leads on, and will forever continue to lead on, the Christian Science movement.

What is the responsibility of her followers? Is it not to go forward—to acknowledge her leadership, heed her counsels, obey her mandates, grow in spiritual understanding, and demonstrate through the spirituality and integrity of their lives the divine Principle she teaches? Christian Science makes no compromise with evil. It offers no excuse for self-indulgence and apathy. Divine

Her prophecies

Principle demands obedience, absolute purity and integrity in thought, word, and deed.

The great lifework of this intrepid Leader continues to bless mankind. With full faith in their love and loyalty she charges Christian Scientists with the task of restraining crime, aiding in the ejection of error, and joyfully proving the victory of good over evil. With unfailing vision and unwavering confidence in God, she sees the universality of Love, the triumph of good, and the final appearing of God's spiritual universe and man.

Those of us who are Christian Scientists need to watch and work and pray that this divine Love may inhabit our hearts and mold our lives. Thus shall we hasten the day promised by Habakkuk when "the earth shall be filled with the knowledge of the glory of the Lord, as the waters cover the sea." [9]

As we meditate upon these things and ponder their deep significance, there may well echo within us the conviction which came to Ezekiel, "And when this cometh to pass, (lo, it will come,) then shall they know that a prophet hath been among them." [10]

[1] The First Church of Christ, Scientist, and Miscellany, p. 127
[2] Ecclesiastes 3:14, 15
[3] Luke 17:21
[4] Science and Health, p. 84;   [5] p. 468
[6] I Corinthians 15:54
[7] Science and Health, p. 174
[8] No and Yes, p. 44
[9] Habakkuk 2:14
[10] Ezekiel 33:33